First published in Great Britain in 2016

British Library Cataloguing-in-Publication Data
A CIP record for this title is available from the British Library

ISBN 978 0 85704 299 6

HALSGROVE
Halsgrove House,
Ryelands Business Park,
Bagley Road, Wellington, Somerset TA21 9PZ
Tel: 01823 653777   Fax: 01823 216796
email: sales@halsgrove.com

Part of the Halsgrove group of companies
Information on all Halsgrove titles is available at: www.halsgrove.com

Printed in the UK by TJ International Ltd

Contents

Preface

I'VE BEEN WRITING now for thirty years, and in one way or another, I've always been writing about my home county, in between other books. There is something about certain English counties that keeps their peculiar magic in the forefront of the media. One only has to think of the phenomenal success of Roy Clarke's *Last of the Summer Wine* to see what it is about Yorkshire that puts it in the rank of the most persistently popular of the shires. It is all about a certain attitude to life, and a disarming, wry humour.

In my fictional guise, writing my Uncle Albert short story collections, I have tapped into this humour and the attitude behind it. My own family, based in Churwell and Beeston, have been fictionalised, at least in part, in those stories. But I am able to write the following tales because as I have grown older I have come to know most corners of the shire known as 'Broad Acres.' For me, there seems to be a never-ending supply of stories from the chronicles, particularly in the Victorian and Edwardian periods. Perhaps that was when the Industrial Revolution was in its second wave and the population growth of the cities – Bradford, Leeds and Sheffield in particular – was tremendously accelerated by the expansion of the conurbations.

Still, the county is somehow always rural in spirit. Growing up in the West Riding, the culture of the working people in my family and community exemplified William Cobbett's insistence that happiness and fulfilment lie in having a patch of land for growing vegetables and a pig. Simplicity and love of a peaceful life, packed with recreational interest stretching to a community spirit, is a key feature of traditional Yorkshire life.

CHAPTER ONE
The Criminal Element

THE COUNTY OF the broad acres has a wild and dark history, and many of the stories from the annals of transgression and law-breaking relate to the more remote places across the expanse of the Ridings. But of course, with the coming of the Industrial Revolution from the late eighteenth century and well into the nineteenth, there was rapid urban growth and huge populations from the countryside moved into the new towns. Where there is an intense gathering of people, working hard and playing hard, there will be crime, and the industrial towns brought with them such matters as increasing drinking, gambling and rough sports: these all played a part in crime. It might be hard to think of a typical Yorkshire crime, but certainly the county has had its share of horrible murders.

I have spent twenty years of my writing life collecting and producing material relating to Yorkshire's criminal past, and that history is teeming with irresistible stories. I have chosen some of the very best for this collection. The tales are not always gruesome: crime brings its own dark humour with it, and incompetence in these trades is more common than skill. Readers might think that criminal history in the county is all a matter of hangings and sufferings, and of course these narratives are there. But in the assemblage of villains and rogues there are some outstanding examples of incompetence and strangeness.

The following are a sample of those tales which present their own ineffable drama.

The Gibbets

The first gibbet tale concerns a highwayman – Spence Broughton. This is a man who could have been a successful farmer, had he stayed on the right side of the law. Broughton had a farm bought for him at Marton, near Sleaford, when he was just twenty-two. He also gathered more wealth when he married a woman who brought money with her, but all this was not enough for this bad seed, a man who was, in the words of his time, a rake and a villain. He began by gambling, and he mixed with bad company, including a certain John Oxley.

With Oxley, contact started with a London fence called Shaw, and soon Broughton and his friend were taking on robberies. They were paid to rob the Rotherham mail, and the two men got to Chesterfield, from where they would begin the attack. Not far from Rotherham, the two men stopped the coach and there was only the post-boy driving; he was tied up and left. The robbers took the bag but there was little worth having – merely one bill of exchange, though that was for a large sum.

While Broughton stayed in Mansfield, Oxley went to London with the bill. His problem was to convert it into money. In London, with the help of Shaw who had set up the job, Oxley saw that it was possible to do the business and walk out with the cash, in this case from a company in Austin Friars. After giving Broughton just £10 initially, Oxley found himself at the point of being pressured for more, and it seems that Broughton was pleased to take another £40.

Of course, now that the two men had come across a simple means of stealing funds, they were out on the road again; they robbed the Cambridge mail this time, and their difficulties began because a provincial bank note was traced – one of a number that the two men had been working hard to spend in order not to be traced. But they were traced after the energetic and sharp activities of a shop-boy. Some Bow Street officers traced the lodgings where Broughton was staying and, after a chase, they cornered him at an inn called The Dog and Duck. Broughton was taken to Bow Street. Their London contact Shaw turned King's evidence and he told the whole story of the robbery at Cambridge and of where and how they had dealt with and hidden the takings. Later, the two men were examined again, and although the post-boy could not identify them, they were remanded in custody. The enterprising and wily Oxley managed to escape from Clerkenwell bridewell; he disappeared into the night and we know nothing more of him. But Broughton was taken north to York. He was tried before Mr Justice Buller at the Spring Assizes in 1792. There was Shaw against him again, and also a man called Close who had assisted in the financial transactions in London. Broughton was told by the judge that there was not ' a shadow of hope' of any mercy.

Spence Broughton was to be hanged, and also gibbeted. He was reported as having faced that sentence with fortitude, and he prepared himself for death, and was reportedly what the authorities would have called 'a model prisoner.' He died with four others on 14 April, 1792, and before he died he said, 'This is the happiest day that I have experienced for some time.' The story of Broughton

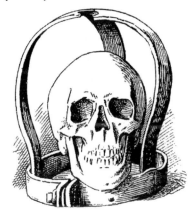

The Hunslet Gibbet

does not end there, however. His body was gibbeted on Attercliffe Common, not far from the Arrow Inn and there was a weekend like a local feast day, with his body being pulleyed up into position on the Monday morning. But some years later, in 1827 a man called Sorby bought the land around the gibbet, and a few years before that, when some of the bones of the highwayman had loosened and fallen, the tale is told of a local potter who took some of the skeleton's fingers and used them to make some bone china items. One of these, a jug, was sold in London in 1871. Such is the notoriety of this Sheffield rogue that over the years, people have hoarded and preserved anything related to his story, and in one of the York archive stores, a piece of the gibbet is still preserved.

The gibbet, once a fearful thing for a condemned man, was either a British version of the guillotine, or a high frame on a pole. The former sliced off the head of a murderer and the latter was a place where a hanged man's bones were left to be picked at by the crows. Yorkshire had her own – in Halifax.

According to J. Horsfall Turner, the Calderdale historian, the gibbet was in Halifax 'since the remotest times, certainly from the conquest of 1066.' There were forty-nine beheadings done there between 1541 and 1650. It was a stone structure, with stone steps. In the early nineteenth century it looked as though there was no trace of the gibbet left, but workmen in 1839 digging in a heap of rubble found a platform, and this was the one on which executions had taken place. This is undoubtedly the most famous gibbet in English history, and today, Gibbet Street still remains on the street-sign.

In the early nineteenth century it looked as though there was no trace of the old gibbet; the wooden frame was assumed to have rotted long ago, and there was no blade anywhere. But workmen in June, 1839 were digging in a heap of rubble and they found a stone platform – the one on which executions took place.

The Halifax historian and biographer of the Brontës, Francis Leyland, was fairly sure he knew where the platform would be, so the workmen perhaps were half expecting the find. At that time, the gibbet had been very much an important piece of interest, as there had been a play produced in 1833 called *Gibbet Laws of Halifax*, written by the local writer, Thomas Crossley, the Ovenden Bard.

The old tale of the gibbet was that if a man about to be beheaded could jump out as he heard the pin being slid out, and if he could run down to the river and across it, then even if the executioner caught him, he could not be brought back to be killed. A story often told is that of a man who managed to do all that, and he was followed by the executioner, and the felon was supposed to have shouted for his hat to be brought to him. Such dark humour always follows a gibbet tale.

There is also the Hunslet gibbet, and thanks to an antiquarian who reported on a collection of strange objects over a century ago now, we have a drawing of this ghastly device. This is a gibbet iron, and the correspondent wrote, in 1900, that his drawing was of a 'skull of a well-known Yorkshire character who paid the penalty for murder, and the gibbet irons in which people of that character were hanged in the 'good old days'. The body was handed over to the medical students... as was the practice in those days, and eventually the skull... was handed to us... The gibbet iron is a substantial piece of work. The hole at the top in which the swivel was placed is distinctly shown, and it is the iron used on the occasion of the last person to be hanged on the gibbet at Hunslet, near Leeds.'

Yorkshire's Own Sherlock

There was no professional detective force in England until 1842, and that was only the start of it, being formed in the Metropolitan Police. But as the century went on and regional forces were formed, there were small detective branches and plain clothes men across the land. It had formerly been common practice to ask Scotland Yard men to come out to the provinces when there was something that was beyond the resources of the regional force, such as Chartist or Luddite problems. There had been special constables and the police of course, but when it came to the special skills of detective work, specialists were needed, and there was no shortage of men keen to acquire the kudos of being sleuths.

The regional detectives in Victorian Britain are not well known, and the publications are few. One Manchester man, who was famous at the time, was Jerome Caminada, who worked mostly in Manchester and who wrote his memoirs at the end of the century. He explained that drink and crime were inextricably mixed: ' Much of my work over 27 years as a detective was aimed at closing down illegal beer houses and putting an end to criminal activities that happened on licensed premises.' He had something of a crusade in his later writings, asking the question, how come the worst criminals are the ones with the longest records?

The new detectives in places like Doncaster and Sheffield had to practise what had been learned in London at the beginning: forming a string of contacts and snitches, using plain clothes disguises, and being as observant as we are asked to believe Sherlock Holmes was. They also had to learn how to cope with the more subtle types of crime – the non-violent ones that involved swindles, frauds and deception.

In the Doncaster area, the detective who stole the limelight in all kinds of contexts was Detective Officer Winn. He was based in Sheffield but often found himself at work in Doncaster and beyond. In 1858 he found himself on the tail of a forger who worked across South Yorkshire, going to horse fairs and passing dud cheques and forged notes. He had the same name as a very famous man of Victorian times – William Morris – and he was caught courtesy of the *Police Gazette*. This publication, still going well today, was originally called *Hue and Cry,* and was circulated across London at first and then further afield, with descriptions of wanted criminals, lists of army deserters and short accounts of crimes.

One day in April, 1858, Detective Wetherall of Sheffield was on the hunt for Morris and when he went into one of the public houses where villains tended to congregate he saw a copy of the *Police Gazette* on a table. It couldn't have been a more significant clue: the publication was folded just as it had arrived, and there was a line drawing of Morris, visible. Wetherall knew that the best bet was that Morris had, through sheer crook's vanity, wanted to see how he was described in print.

It didn't take long to find out that Morris was lodging in a room upstairs and was in his room at that moment. Issuing false bank notes was a very serious offence: thirty years before this, it had been a hanging offence and even in the 1850s it had a likely sentence of many years penal servitude. In those days when the police communication was still with whistles or feet, Wetherall had to run to the nearest police station for help. He knew that Officer Winn was a good man and he was there, so the two detectives went to get their man. They were soon entering the room where Morris was sitting. Wetherall identified him as the man he was searching for, and Winn at once seized him.

Detectives Winn and Wetherall knew that Morris had tried to drop a parcel in the corner of the room, and when they retrieved it, they found a roll of forged notes. Winn looked closely at them, and he knew that apparently they were cleverly done, with a correct watermark and excellent reproduction. But the officer's skilful eye could see that they were forged. Morris also had a bag of forged sovereigns on him, called 'jacks'

The full story about Morris came out then: he had been a convict for many years and had returned on a ticket of leave. His life was transient and reckless, even though he had married recently – to a woman he had known only a short time.

Also in Sheffield, Winn collared another man who had been at work around Doncaster, and who had called at a butcher's saying he had several 'fat beasts' for sale. The normal price would have been around £20 but the man was asking for just six pounds. Clearly, this was a case of stolen cattle being shifted very quickly, and the rogue would have moved on elsewhere with a quick profit. The man was to gather his animals in the Sheffield

Shambles and sell them there: Winn had learned that from a contact. The detective was soon there, in plain clothes, and he took the man in charge and had the cattle taken to the Yellow Lion.

George Winn was becoming a very smart professional by the early 1860s. In 1864 he was involved in one of his most high-profile cases, and one of Doncaster's most large scale burglaries in the nineteenth century. The crooks in the case were George Harris and George Perry from Huddersfield; they travelled across Yorkshire, 'casing' likely easy targets for burglary, and then worked as a team. They were adroit and cunning, and planned the work well, but on this occasion they met Winn and were taken into custody.

On the 12th September in this year the two men loitered on Christchurch Terrace by a house owned by a Miss Drabwell. She had gone away for a while to stay with her niece, but left her niece to look in and check the property when she could. But on the 20th the police were told that there had been 'an extensive burglary' there. Miss Drabwell was telegraphed and informed and she returned.

The thieves had broken into the house from the rear and then worked recklessly through the place, ransacking everything and going from room to room. Miss Drabwell was wealthy, and she kept a wine cellar. The thieves had discovered this and had a good time. Police found that several bottles had been drunk, two bottles of brandy had also been drunk, and the burglars had also smoked cigars there. As to the booty the crooks went away with, the list was massive, including silver spoons, candlesticks, a silk mantle, silk jackets, a cashmere tablecloth and all kinds of silver items. They had also found and taken 30 yards of satin and all kinds of jewellery. But the burglars had a 'fence' called Charles Walker, and detectives kept an eye on him. Sure enough, at a shop belonging to a Mr Cash in Sheffield, a man who was working with the burglars went in and offered two seals. These had a crest on them, and Mr Cash was suspicious. Cash was used to helping police catch up with the rogues trying to unload their booty, so he asked the man to come back with more items and he would buy them as a job lot. But Cash also told police and who was waiting for the man in the afternoon? George Winn. Charles Walker came to the shop, with the burglars behind; Walker had a bag under his coat, and Winn grabbed him. The other crooks ran away. But Walker spilled the beans under pressure and led Winn and officers to the lodging house where all the stolen goods were kept.

What is particularly interesting in the way the case ends, and the success of the hunt for the Doncaster burglars, is the Yorkshire detective network. The burglars returned to Huddersfield but descriptions had been sent on, and police were waiting for them. They were in the dock at Doncaster police court and sent on to Leeds Assizes, and from there to a long time behind bars.

We have a confirmation of Caminada's comments about drink and crime. When any kind of new or refurbished pub or 'eating house' was established, it was checked out. Obviously, known criminals would always be out to settle in a fresh den, and often with a 'legitimate' front. Winn was often the man called in to help give these places a clean bill of health in terms of criminal potential. A typical example was the Alexandra Music Hall in Sheffield, where the magistrates were opposing a licence to the owner who was trying to import foreign wines. Winn was called; he had clearly been to visit the place and also walked past it at different times of day, and he gave testimony to say that he had no grounds to be suspicious of the owner and staff.

This shows that the new detectives in the shires were powerful, influential men in some areas of urban life; the career of George Winn, Detective Officer, shows just how adaptable and resourceful these officers had to be, dealing both with the usual physical force side of policing and with white collar crime in that restless, pushy society which was opening up all kinds of new areas of crime as population expanded and industry diversified.

Ripper Tales Up North

In the 'Ripper year' of 1888, there was a flood of hoax letters to the police. Clearly, such hoaxes are a very stupid and dangerous activity. The culprits are very difficult to track down, but Bradford appears to be the only place in which a writer of such a letter was caught and charged. She was Maria Coroner, a Canadian-born milliner living in Westgrove Street, a woman with a dark side. She had written to the local newspaper and to the Chief Constable, saying when caught that she had done it as a joke, and the whole affair attracted a large media interest when she appeared in court on 23 October that year.

Maria was fined £20 and bound over to keep the peace for six months. One newspaper report said that 'a dense crowd fought for admission to the court.' It has disturbing echoes of Wearside Jack and the Yorkshire Ripper hoax in our own time. But in an age when the popular press made great sensational tales out of commonplace domestic killings, the strange twisted fantasy that produces 'Ripper letters' can to a certain extent be understood.

The Maria Coroner case was a curiosity, but we can add to that something far more startling and intriguing that happened in Bradford that year – it may have been the Ripper himself who came north to kill, and perhaps after taunting the metropolitan Police with his own terrible letters.

Just after Christmas, 1888, John Gill of Thorncliff Road, went for a ride on a milk cart. It was very early in the morning, and his mother never saw him alive again. He had been seen playing but also, menacingly, he was seen talking to a man, a stranger to the area by all accounts. The family soon felt the distress of his absence, and feared the worst; they placed a poster on view, with a physical description of him, and actually used the word 'lost' despite the fact that it was only a day after his disappearance.

John, eight years old, was found in a stable by Joe Buckle, a butcher. Joe was cleaning the place when he saw a pile of some indescribable objects, and looking closer, he saw that it was a corpse, and most noticeable on first inspection was the fact that one ear had been sliced off. He ran for help. Later, when a closer inspection was made by officers, it was found that there had been extreme mutilation of the body; his stomach had been cut open and vital organs placed on top of him. He had been repeatedly cut, stabbed in the chest, and there was a rough noose around his neck. This is where the complex business of the massive number of Ripper letters figure in the story. The pathology certainly makes the Gill murder a contender for being classified as a Ripper killing; Dr Bond in London, when writing about the body of victim Mary Kelly, noted that 'the viscera were found in various parts... the liver between the feet and the spleen by the left side of the body.' There are similarities, but the main argument for the Ripper coming north rests on the statements made in the letters. As Philip Sugden has written, 'The important question is... whether any of these letters we have noticed was written by the murderer.' This was said about the first letter received, well before the Bradford case. By the time of the Gill killing, police were walking into Whitechapel in pairs and detectives were everywhere around the area. Five killings had taken place in London, the last in November, just a month before the Bradford case.

At the end of November, one of the Ripper letters had the text, 'I shall do another murder on some young youth such as printing lads who work in the city. I did write you once before... I shall do them worse than the women, I shall take their hearts...' The crime writer, Patricia Cornwell, believes that the Bradford murder is worth serious consideration. But the problem with Patricia Cornwell's use of the Ripper letters in associating the Bradford case with Jack is that she talks of the 'Ripper letter' as if their provenance is certified and that certain examples cluster together as the work of individual authors (see her book, *Portrait of a Killer*). This is why she dismisses the most tantalising scrap of detail in poor John Gill's murder: that a piece of a Liverpool newspaper was used to wrap part of the body. Even more fascinating, the paper had a name on it: 'W. Mason, Derby Road.'

Those ripperologists who think that the mystery killer was James Maybrick, merchant of Liverpool, would perhaps point to the fact that Maybrick was most probably meeting someone in Manchester at one point in 1888, but otherwise, apparently never went near Bradford. Recent writing on Maybrick, and notably the new work done by handwriting and paper experts on the celebrated book, *The Diaries of Jack the Ripper* would seem to confirm that there is no factual evidence for the Bradford connection. We have known for a long time that there was a Lancashire connection, because of James Bierley from Rochdale, who was linked to the Maybrick family.

The Ripper letters in the hand of the painter Walter Sickert, whom Cornwell believes to have been the Ripper, also contain one text that reads, 'I riped[sic] up a little boy in Bradford.' The great Sherlock Holmes would have reacted to this by insisting that, though these Bradford letters may have been by the same hand, there is nothing to prove that they belonged to the man we know as Jack the Ripper. In other words, what we most likely have here is that well-known phenomenon in homicide, the copycat crime.

Bradford was, as Patricia Cornwell points out, a city on the tour being made by the great actor, Sir Henry Irving, and Sickert had been an actor, and was fond of playgoing. If he had gone north to distract affairs from Whitechapel, as Cornwell points out, ' Many of the cities mentioned in the Ripper letters were on Henry Irving's theatre company's schedule, which was published in the newspapers daily…' The same is said in her book about race courses, another passion of Sickert's, and of course, it is not difficult to find race courses near Bradford in 1888. This is all speculation, but interesting nevertheless.

The existence of the Bradford references open up new possibilities, but beneath all the hype and speculation, we have the existence of such copycat crimes and the psychology of serial killing now very much established in academic study. The thought behind killer profiling does not find satisfactory lines of thought in the Gill murder. It is not convincing that the sexual-sadistic Ripper would switch to murders of young men, and also the use of the noose is bizarre as a scene of crime ritual communication, as such killers tend to do. Another curious detail on Gill's body was a piece of torn shirting about his neck – again, hardly a signature of the Ripper in London. As far as the Bradford connection is concerned, the events could have turned out tragically for the prime local suspect, one Bill Barrett, the dairyman, but he was cleared and had had 'a long interview' with his legal adviser that was undoubtedly the basis of a sound defence. The only evidence was circumstantial. If the killing was a copycat murder, then the identity of the real killer remains a mystery, and the Gill case is in the annals of unsolved crimes.

The Bradford case is not the only one that may be another Ripper victim outside Whitchapel. In June, 1887, at Temple Stairs on the Thames, parts of a body previously found at Rainham were found in a parcel. At the inquest it was asserted that someone with a knowledge of anatomy had done this ghastly murder. Eventually, as in this Bradford scenario, a letter supposedly from the 'real' Ripper denied any involvement with these body parts. At least the Bradford killing had some definite pointers to the actual Ripper.

Eugene Aram

Few criminal tales from Yorkshire's past have captured the imagination more than this of the Knaresborough schoolmaster whose destiny was the hangman's rope. In the 1870s, such was the power of his story that one writer could comment, 'The house in which he was born has long since been destroyed to its foundations; the sight is however pointed out on a piece of unoccupied ground in the rear of two new cottages. In one of the latter is a relic, which tradition invariably attributes to him, a carving in stone of a large human face... The nose is broken and it is otherwise mutilated... it is now placed for better preservation above the fire-place in the kitchen of one of the new cottages.' This is a perfect example of the Victorian fascination with everything attaching to the macabre, and indeed, it is a habit which has lasted into modernity, along with this tale of murder.

The story of schoolmaster Eugene Aram and a mysterious death in Knaresborough is arguably Yorkshire's most mysterious unsolved case of murder. That may seem a strange thing to say, given that Aram was sentenced for the murder of Daniel Clarke and subsequently hanged; but the truth is that there are several doubts about Aram's guilt. It is tempting to suggest that enemies wanted him charged and out of the way; after all, a former friend gave evidence against him, and that evidence clearly made the man, Houseman, an accessory.

Aram was born in Netherdale in 1704 and he was something of a prodigy of self-education. His father was merely a gardener, but Aram was clearly destined for a career in the field of learning and education; he spent some time in London as a bookkeeper and then came home, to Knaresborough in 1734 where he gained some experience as a tutor. Later he became a schoolmaster and moved to Lynn in Norfolk. We are asked to believe that a learned gentleman with a good income would mix with characters of disreputable character, because a murder was committed some time within the period between Aram being employed in Knaresborough in 1734 and the finding of a body in 1758. In that year a labourer digging ground to make a lime-kiln at Thistle Hill found a human skeleton. At the coroner's inquest, someone stated that fourteen years before, a man called Daniel Clarke, had disappeared without a trace. The names of Aram and Houseman were linked to Clarke, as they had been friendly at the time.

That is where the drama of this case began: Aram was traced to Lynn and arrested, then brought back to Yorkshire for trial. He stood trial at the York Assizes. But all writing about the alleged murder since has focused on the crucially important questions such as whose was the body? There was no proof it was Clarke's. Also, the testimony of Houseman, who was the main witness called against Aram at York, was clearly biased and untrustworthy. In addition, so-called evidence was all circumstantial. But perhaps most remarkable of all was the fact that Aram conducted his own defence.

At that time (and not until 1896) the accused could not speak except in response to the judge's call for 'anything to say' at the end, before sentence was passed. Aram acted for himself and did a thoroughly efficient job of it. The narrative that emerged about Aram as he was in 1734 is one that suggests Aram, Clarke and Houseman were often together; that Aram's marriage had been a failure and his wife had become an implacable enemy against her former husband. These factors became part of the tale of guilt put together by Houseman. He claimed that the three men had exploited the fact that Clarke had 'come into money' when he married; valuables were gathered on credit, based on his wife's income (so Houseman said). Then, thieves fell out, and Houseman claimed that he had seen Aram batter Clarke to death in a field as they walked in front of him, and that was on a February evening. Aram rightly argued that Houseman would not have been behind them but walking with them, to an important meeting, and also that on a dark February evening, he would not have seen such a thing. Another important detail was that Aram had had a very serious illness at that time, leaving his face scarred and his whole constitution weakened.

The most persuasive reasoning in Aram's own defence covered such things as his lack of a motive in doing such an awful deed, and that his basic character and temperament did not ft well with such a murderous act. Aram said of himself: 'Could such a person in this condition take anything into his head so unlikely, so extravagant? I, past the vigour of my age, feeble and valetudinary, with no inducement to engage, no ability to accomplish, no weapon wherewith to perpetrate such a fact; without interest, without power, without motive, without means…'

He also destroyed whatever medical and forensic details might have been deduced from the found skeleton. He sensibly said that it could have been anyone, from any time. But all this was of no use. Judge Noel was impressed, but there was no material change in attitudes. Aram was thrown upon the mercy of the court and the jury found him guilty.

In gaol at York, he attempted suicide, trying to cut his arm with a razor; yet we have, as Lord Birkenhead pointed out long ago, a mystery in that a second letter alleging to be by Aram was found, and it was one that had clearly been fabricated by someone. We do know that Aram wrote some last words and also a poem. He said ' Though I am now stained by malevolence and suffer by prejudice, I hope to rise fair and unblemished. My life was not polluted, my morals irreproachable, and my opinions orthodox.

Eugene Aram was hanged at York on 6 August, in a most pathetic state, mainly through the loss of blood he had suffered; his wrists were bound and blood-stained. The ultimate insult to this man who may have been a killer but who has never had any solid evidence set against him, was that his

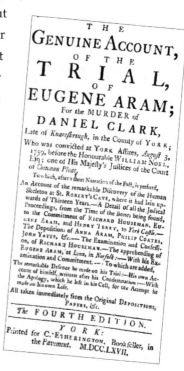

Cover of a popular publication on Eugene Aram York Museums Trust

body was suspended in chains in Knaresborough forest – a kind of gibbeting done to deter other potential malefactors.

An interesting coda to the story is that a woman in 1837 who was living in an almshouse at Wisbech told a writer for *The Gentleman's Magazine* that she had been a girl when Aram was arrested at Lynn and she saw him at the time. She said that the boys of the school had been in tears at the arrest, so much was Aram esteemed by them. The most interesting note from her memory was that she said Aram turned bodily when looking behind him – never merely turning his head. The writer in 1890 who recorded this, added, 'Has any poet, any observer of nature, ever depicted this instance of fear mustering up resolution?' The writer, R. V. Taylor, appears to be trying to suggest that Aram exhibited some kind of possible guilt and fear. As with everything connected with this tragic tale, the truth will never be out.

Aram's poem has some of the most stoical and impressive lines ever written from the death-cell:

> 'Calm and composed, my soul her journey takes,
> No guilt that troubles, and no heart that aches.
> Adieu thou Sun; all bright like her arise;
> Adieu fair friends, and all that's good and wise.'

As a writer commenting on the case in 1880 noted, 'The whole affair is enveloped in mystery and it will ever remain so... but is it not possible, after all, that Eugene Aram fell a victim to a vile conspiracy, got up by a set of designing and unprincipled villains, with whom in the unsuspecting simplicity of his heart, he had occasionally associated.'

Strange Meeting in Dartmoor

Sometimes, in researching crime stories, the tale comes to a definite conclusion, but the villain or victim in question is committed to oblivion and no more is heard of them. But in this story, a murderer from Doncaster who went to jail for the murder of his wife, and so to an anonymous prison life, happened to meet a famous Irishman, and so the end of his tale is available to historians. This is a rare event in criminal history.

On 11 July, around six o'clock, Thomas Slack, aged forty, came home from a long drinking session; he found his wife, Ann, also drunk. They lived at the Holmes in Wheatley. A little girl had been helping Ann do some housework, and she left just before Thomas appeared on the scene. The house had a kitchen and a front room, and later it was ascertained where exactly Slack struck – for he did strike, just minutes after coming home. He went into a rage when seeing her drunk: he took out his pocket knife and stabbed her in the neck. Ann staggered outside, screaming for help. She was bleeding heavily of course, and she fell as she went outside, into the arms of a neighbour who had rushed to the spot.

The woman who first held the dying woman was Hannah Slack (aunt by marriage to the prisoner) and she left Ann breathing her last, with another woman before going inside and confronting the man. Hannah found him in the front room sitting on a sofa with his hand in his pocket and she said,

'You have murdered your wife!'

Slack answered, 'I have not seen her, where is she?' But the drunk strangely then added, 'Oh is she dead? She was my best friend… I'm very sorry.'

Hannah Slack now emerges as the heroine in the tale. The hand in his pocket grasped his knife and he said that he was going to take his own life. Hannah restrained him and shouted for help. It was very risky for her to have gone in there alone, in the first place. The other neighbours around responded and finally came to her assistance. Slack was grabbed and held, and a short time after the police arrived, led by Superintendent Astwood, who arrested Slack and took him away. He was charged with murder but he was sober enough to say that it was not so, because he was in drink. That was significant, because at court he stood indicted on charges of both murder and manslaughter.

The definition of murder needs to be placed at this point in the sad story: a murder is a killing with is done 'with malice aforethought' – there has to be a *mens rea* – an aim to kill – and then the *actus reus* – the deed done which would lead to the taking of life. The two Latin terms are crucially important. Slack had immediately thought that his drunkenness would be a defence and would pre-empt a murder charge. He was wrong.

Dr Charles Fenton gave medical evidence, saying he arrived on the scene about forty five minutes after the deadly attack. He found a wound two inches long on Ann's neck; this was close to the left ear and death had been caused by the piercing of the carotid artery.

It was clear from this that the knife wound had caused the death.

It was looking bleak for Slack. His defence, Mr Price Q.C., straightaway introduced the notion of provocation, saying, 'I have known and worked with the family for several years… Mr Slack is a good and kind husband. The deceased was very unkind and provoking in every sense of the word. She did not bear a good character.'

Price then launched into the high drama of the plea aimed at the jury, insisting that this had not been wilful murder. He said, cleverly, that the law was bound to lay down general principles, but the application of these principles lay with the jury…' In other words, he was angling for the wilful murder to be dropped by reason of severe provocation. The argument was that Price had suffered long and hard over the years, worthily trying to bring this fallen woman back to habits of sobriety.

But Hannah Slack's testimony was crucially important. Slack had some barges on the River Don and Hannah pointed out that he was often away from home; their marriage was a very unhappy one, she said. Then she described how she had seen both of them very drunk on that fateful evening. After the killing but before Hannah had known, she saw Slack walking along the garden and he 'doubled up his hands and ruffled his hair in quite a delirious manner.'

Price was stretching all sinews and brain cells to paint a good picture of Slack. He cross-examined Hannah and she explained, 'He has had to call me up dozens of times when he could not get deceased to bed because she was so drunk… I have often seen men come to the house when he has been away.' The tale of their life together was depressing. Hannah pointed out that when the Slacks were first married they had a well-furnished house. ' Drink had led Ann to pawn absolutely everything for beer or gin-money, and Hannah pointed out that there was not even a blanket in the house to put over the deceased body.

It was apparent that the man had been driven to distraction, and the presiding judge, Mr Justice Lowe, asked Price if he intended to set up an insanity defence. The answer was no: he was keeping to the provocation appeal.

The Slacks had been married for ten years, but for the last six months the decline had been extreme. Hannah said that Slack had been going to Sheffield almost every day in that period, and coming home drunk, finding yet more items pawned and both of them heading for complete destitution.

There was no doubt about the version of events given at the first statement of the events: Mary Humprey, a neighbour, testified that she had held Ann as she died, and confirmed that she was very intoxicated. Thomas Bramworth, another neighbour, came to the scene and he recalled saying, 'Slack, whatever have you done?' and the man had replied:

'Do save her life and take mine… she was the best friend I had!'

Superintendent Astwood confirmed that Slack had denied murder when in custody in Doncaster. So what was the situation at that point? It was that Slack was being painted for the jury as a man distracted, one who although he had a severe drink problem himself, he was possibly stretched to mental instability all because of his wife. In other words, there was no talk of his actions causing the relationship to deteriorate and no account of his failure to act with regard to the financial worries – all he had done was spend more.

The jury found Slack guilty of manslaughter. But the judge had a shock in store for Slack and for Price, his barrister.

The judge summed up with an oblique and vague reference to potential human understanding of Slack's situation: he said, 'I am quite sure that both the jury and myself would gladly give effect to any circumstances if they could do so consistently with their duty.' But there was a word from his mouth that had a tone of foreboding for Slack: he said 'But…' His final words were:

> *'The jury has taken a very merciful view of this case. There was no doubt that it was a moral murder, although legally manslaughter. If any circumstances should arise, either as regarded his health or otherwise, they must be the subject of an application to a higher authority. But I feel it right, for an offence of this kind, although committed in a moment of drunkenness and repented afterwards, to have a sentence of twenty years penal servitude.'*

This was a bombshell in the court. The sentence was, in those times, virtually a sentence to a future of a 'living death.' Slack would enter a limbo in which he would move from hard labour and fearful discipline into such a drain of his self-identity that should he live to the age of sixty and complete the sentence, he would be a broken man.

Through the whole trial, Slack had been in a posture of prayer and was indeed heard to mumble words. He had been given permission to sit, as he was not well. But that modicum of consideration was something that must have misled all present with regard to the nature of this judge. In the end, a life had been taken with intent. The judge knew that, and that is what he meant by 'moral murder.' He found a way to defeat and deflect the jury's decision into something that he personally knew was justice.

A woman in the low condition of the poor deceased, however aggressive and difficult, deserved a husband who would try to help, try to change things for the better – not a man who would take her life in a drunken rage.

Half-Hanged Smith

Usually, a death sentence back in the horrendous days of hanging, meant the end. There was no way back into the world. But strangely, for a select few, that was not the case, and the noose and scaffold were not the last scene to meet their eyes on this earth.

The hero of this story may have had the most ordinary of names – John Smith – but his story is extraordinary in the extreme. Smith served at sea on a man o'war after being apprentice in London to a packer. After that he joined the army and was in a guards regiment, but he was always destined for a life of crime and fell into bad company.

Smith was active as a thief at a time when over two hundred capital crimes were on the statute books, so it was not difficult at that time for a villain to find himself on a journey to the scaffold at Tyburn. Smith stood against five indictments and indeed the judge put on the black cap and sentenced him to death.

To Tyburn he went, with the usual crowd gathering. The stages in the familiar ritual took place: the slow drive down Oxford Street and the arrival at the hanging tree. Then the speeches from the scaffold and the expected repentance or defiance. Smith appeared to be fond of a dying speech but was not really openly concerned about being 'turned off' and he was hanged. At that time, the art of hanging was an uncertain business and the hangmen were usually drunks and criminals doing the distasteful work to gain their own remission or even freedom.

Consequently, Smith had been dangling and fighting for life on the end of the rope for some minutes when a voice cried, ' A reprieve!' He was cut down. Fortunately, he had no close friends or family, because if he had, they would have pulled and swung on his legs to hasten his end.

Smith was asked what it felt like to be strangled by a drunk and he said, 'When I was turned off I was sensible for some time of a very great pain, as my body is weighty... I felt my spirits to be in a great commotion, and I saw a great blaze, a blinding light which seemed to go out of my eyes with a flash, then I lost all sense of pain.

The lucky man was back to his life of crime, though, and once again before the judge and jury. But at the Old Bailey for house-breaking, there was a special verdict and he walked free. On the third trial in his life, after again robbing the good citizens of London, he would almost certainly have been to Tyburn again, except that the prosecutor died before the trial began. The commentators at the time considered it fitting that he should turn to Christ and leave off his criminal career, after such special providential care of his life. But it seems unlikely that he stopped his burglaries.

Smith was the son of a Malton farmer in North Yorkshire. His parents and relatives must have read about him, such was his short-lived fame. But none came to see him die, as far as we know, and if they had done, he would have certainly have died.

No Mary Evans...

The drawing compels attention: a young woman having a noose secured around her neck as she listens to a podgy clergyman holding a prayer book; a repulsive hangman grasps the knot of rope on her neck. His expression is a foul leer, a facial expression conveying a perverted delight in seeing the girl 'stretched.' Her coffin stands behind her. Beneath we have the words, ' Mary Evans, hung at York Aug. 10th 1799 for poisoning her husband...' The signature below the coffin is simply 'Rowlandson.' The image is harsh, explicit, and relates to all that body of hanging literature which made men rich on the streets when they sold chapbooks and broadsides about the gory deaths and noisy repentances on the scaffold.

What kind of imagination could conceive of such a thing? Was it a twisted and vicarious vision of pain by a mind sick with the sexual kick such an image might give a perverted mind? Why imagine such a despicable thing? I was amazed when the artist turned out to be someone who, while showing a profound interest in all aspects of the criminal justice system of his time, was quite clearly not a horrendous deviant, and was in fact a man who saw and represented the worst aspects of 'man's inhumanity to man' which he saw around him. After all, as I discovered, he would have been a man who, until Tyburn was not used any longer for executions in 1800, would have seen the cart with the condemned person rolling along the streets of London outside his home. A quick glance at a biographical summary told me that the artist was a Londoner, and that he would have known the city very well. This raised the question of whether he knew York. Not only did I speculate that he imagined the hanging, but he may have imagined York. The city was well known for York Castle of course. John Palmer, alias Dick Turpin had been hanged at York in 1739. No doubt Rowlandson, as a boy, had heard mention of the villain's name and read about him in the street ballads and chap books of the time.

That was not my first encounter with this remarkable artist. I am a crime historian and his work is everywhere to be found in works of social history. But this work arrested the attention. I had to know more, and when I researched my book, *Hanged at York* in 2008, I naturally tried to follow up the narrative in that image. But the problem was that there was no such hanging, and nor was there a Mary Evans hanged at York. The information below the drawing is precise, a date given and a name, with an offence. Yet it was all a fabrication, a flash of grim imaginative depiction, naturally of a scene that would often be seen at York at that time, but certainly not a document of fact. That made the image all the more fascinating – that it was not apparently fact, but imaginative projection, done with what aim? To shock, to wallow in vicarious pleasure? It had to be made by someone who felt a need to express the horror within the surface simplicity: what was just another job for the hangman was a significant event for the artist and for his need to betray his society for what it was – callous, inhumane and stained with corruption and violence.

Strangely, that anomaly did not deter me at all: in fact it heightened my interest in the man who drew it. The artist had to be a man who wanted to point out a gross cruelty, the very essence of man's inhumanity to man. In fact, just ten years before the date given on the drawing, a wife who poisoned her husband would not have been hanged – she would have been burned at the stake, because her crime would have been petty treason, not murder. In other words, the society in which Thomas Rowlandson lived was barbarous and heartless to its transgressors. Yet it was also a society in which 'manners' were highly valued and its literature suggests the genteel world of Jane Austen and the 'men of feeling' in the novels of the 1790s, following Henry Mackenzie's best-seller of that title. Rowland-son, as a man desiring to show the world its own heartless self, was an intriguing figure. Suddenly, all the images of dangerous travel, accidents in the street, fat men and women filling up with ale, grotesque couplings and bloated bodies, fell into place. They were parts of a steady, unified vision of a world brimming with human dynamism, sometimes killing its own and sometimes celebrating life and its giddy sensuality.

Surely there was a biography of this man? That was my question to myself as these thoughts grew. One would expect such a creative soul to be steeped in the life around him, to be known by many, and to be the subject of a thousand memoirs and anecdotes. But no, he was a shadowy figure. The fact is that Rowlandson was always too busy to do what Joseph Conrad advised, to immerse oneself in the 'destructive element' of life with all its pains and struggles, joys and horrors. I then found out that he had squandered an immense fortune at the gaming tables. He was very much a man of his time: a Regency rake without the dandy, and a passionate man without the commitment. But yes, there is a biography now – *Rowlandson's Human Comedy.*

Rowlandson's painting of the hanging that never was.
York Museums and Art Galleries

William Meeke Loses Most of his House

Riots have been a feature of British history since records began, and they have been caused by everything from food shortages to election conflicts. In eighteenth and early nineteenth century Yorkshire they were particularly common, and they were often extremely violent. In the years 1756-1757 for instance, there were over 140 food riots in England and Wales. In a period before any proper regular and professional police, destruction could be horrendously severe. Such was the case in York in 1757. It was all the result of some new legislation – the Militia Act.

Cheaply printed broadsides were the popular media of the time, relishing true crime stories and unexplained events, and the trouble in York was reported by such publications. The Militia Act was terribly unfair, because rich folk could buy themselves out of the service. The mid and late Georgian years were a time in which there were threats of invasion from France particularly, and militia were needed to cope with coastal patrols and with any other emergency. The ordinary man, with no financial resources, could be conscripted for three years – time away from family and business that could ruin him.

In 1788, a writer, Francis Drake, wrote a vivid account of the riot. It all started when, in the wapentake of Bulmer, by Bootham Bar, a meeting was gathering at which the local constables were compiling their conscription lists. A massive crowd assembled, with the express purpose of attacking these constables; Drake wrote, 'they proceeded in a large body, armed with clubs and other unlawful weapons, some on horseback and others on foot, through Monk Bar to the Cockpit House... Not meeting with the deputy lieutenants as expected, they forced the lists from such constables as were in attendance, and after drinking all the liquors in the house, they gutted and pulled it down. They the proceeded to Mr Bowes' house, on the opposite side of the street... which they also gutted and destroyed.

The rampage continued and other property was destroyed. Matters escalated to such a degree that the mayor managed to gather a citizen force of 500 men to counteract the riot. Slowly and steadily, punishment and retribution was to follow, and these punishments included a death penalty and a sentence of transportation. But it took years for the legal process to continue and to be resolved. As late as 1759, there were still poor victims clamouring for redress from the authorities, and one of these was a certain William Meeke, who had suffered grievously in the riots, having most of his property damaged and destroyed. He was demanding around £150 as reparation for this, and in modern values that is approximately £3000. But the damages were never paid.

It was a fairly typical instance of the consequences of criminal actions in mid-eighteenth-century Britain; lawlessness was rife. After all, this was the time of Dick Turpin's depredations, and of the succession of repressive 'Murder Acts' which the government imposed. By 1820 there were to be around 220 capital offences on the statute books.

William Meeke must have felt a deep sense of wrong and injustice, along with many of his neighbours, after that September day when the frustrations and anger of the York mob were let loose, in response to yet another imposition of injustice from the distant government all that way south in Westminster. It would have been a case of that common Yorkshire habit, seen throughout history, of blaming 'the Southerners' for most wrongs. Although, as records show, there were street disturbances in response to the 1757 Act in seven other counties, including Cambridgeshire and Hertfordshire.

Throttled

What greater terror could the poor theatre-goer of the Mid-Victorian times have than the fear that someone would stalk him from behind, wait until there were protective shadows in the street, and then choke him while an accomplice robbed him? Such was the case in many of Britain's cities at the time of a great crisis – the death of Prince Albert in 1861. Matters were glum enough without these street fears, and Yorkshire had its fair share of the villainy.

Up to 17 July, 1862 there had been only fifteen robberies with violence that year in the city of London. But then a Member of Parliament, one Hugh Pilkington, was 'garotted' in Pall Mall. A new and terrifying crime against the person had been noted. In its chronicle of November, 1862, The *Annual Register* reported that there had been a 'garotte terrorism' in London and in the provinces that year. The word 'garotte' was beginning to strike terror into ordinary people and newspapers were selling on headlines about this new version of street robbery. The report expresses the crime in this way:

> *For some years past there have been occasional instances of 'garotte robberies' – a method of highway plunder, which consists in one ruffian seizing an unsuspecting traveller by the neck and crushing in his throat, while another simultaneously rifles his pocket; the scoundrels then decamp, leaving their victim on the ground writhing in agony…*

The popular magazine, *Punch*, covered the menace with its usual acuteness and dash; one cartoon shows some middle-class theatre-goers venturing out into the streets with a platoon of soldiers guarding them. It was nothing less than a reign of terror and it gradually became much more widespread than simply London's theatre land. This 'modern peril of the streets' was first described graphically as 'putting the hug on' and it had its own jargon, the gang members having particular roles. First, the man called the *front stall*, a look-out; then the *back stall* who was going to grab the booty, and finally the *nasty man* who would move in from behind to take the victim's throat. At the time, it was seen as a variety of crime that was somehow not 'British' and journalists tried to blame it on foreigners. It was often written about in terms linked to activities by Italian mobs. But soon it was realised that this heinous crime was becoming a speciality of the new criminal underclass of the expanding towns across Victorian England.

The terror even entered the realms of popular song, with lines such as:

> *A gentleman's walking, perchance with a crutch*
> *he'll suddenly stagger and totter;*
> *don't think that the gentleman's taken too much*
> *he's unluckily met a garrotter…*

In the provinces the new crime began to take a hold towards the late summer of the year. 1862 was destined to become a proper *annus horribilis* for good people on the city streets, and northern towns were no exception. In Sheffield, one of the first notorious garrotters outside London was Edward Hall, a man who was apprehended after a desperate struggle with police. It was reported at the time that he was 'the leader of a gang of ruffians who garrotted and nearly murdered Mr Burnby, Earl Fitzwilliam's coal agent.' He was cornered and surrounded, then jumped from a high window in his home in Sheffield, to escape. But in Birmingham he was grabbed and almost killed by a huge police officer who punched the villain relentlessly until he gave in.

In Bradford, the Chief police officer, Frederick Granhan, was about to be busy with this new type of robbery and his constables' truncheons were going to be needed more than ever. Characters like Hall began to appear in other parts of Yorkshire, and Bradford began to have its share of nasty street attacks by September this year. The streets of the city and the suburbs were indeed perilous at this time. A man was severely bitten by a dog in Grafton Street; he almost had his leg amputated. A fishmonger in Keighley was robbed in broad daylight on his way back from a lunchtime tipple.

A more serious attack took place at Jerusalem in Thornton, where Joe Savile was attacked and robbed by two desperadoes who came across their victim at Well Heads. The attackers, James Jennings and William Shaw, showed no mercy; Jennings took the man's legs tight while Shaw grabbed his neck, then they ripped his coat off and somehow he fought free. As the poor man ran off the robbers shouted that they would catch him and 'kill him off'. Amazingly, though, the accused were acquitted because of lack of any clear accounts by witnesses.

Garotter gangs were not so lucky, and the full weight of the law fell on them. William Holes and James Lynas were in court for their garotte attack on William Dawson late on a Saturday night in Market Street. Dawson, an engine tenter, yelled for the police to help, and an officer came to the scene, to see the two robbers running away down Kirkgate. Holmes was trapped in an alley. Lynas was taken in Collier Gate by a detective called Milnes. They had taken a few shilling and a silk handkerchief. At York Assizes they were to pay dearly for that attack, with a long prison sentence and hard labour waiting for them.

In Calverley, on the moor, a Mr Summerscales was having his constitutional walk when he was set upon by two thugs called Elvidge and Hainsworth. They had used the established methods of one man behind to choke the victim while the other approached face to face, and they had taken his silver watch. But on this occasion, the victim could not positively identify the men and they lived to attack again.

Two hardened toughs called Lockwood and Murphy were one of the most successful garotting teams around Leeds and Bradford, and they became adept at the nefarious business; they had a cover as street hawkers, one selling oysters and the other sold nuts. They trod the streets around the whole conurbation, and were finally tracked down after an attack in Hunslet, though they had been active in Armley and Bingley. Murphy was the 'nasty man' and appears to have been extremely threatening and

dangerous. It is not difficult to see how this crime would catch on in the criminal ranks; it reached the proportions of being a 'glamour' offence in that in took skill, a brazen attitude and a total lack of fear. Lockwood and Murphy almost beat their last victim to death, and they took a trip to York Assizes where they were due to suffer physical punishment and years inside.

'The Garotter's Friend' Punch

The press began to speculate about how the most likely recruits to the garotting craze were ticket-of-leave men. These were convicts whose terms of sentence had been lifted after good behaviour, so that they could go into society to work, though they were required to attend musters, just as today we have a licence system in the current penal code. A ticket could be granted after the prisoner had served at least three years. Penal servitude had replaced the use of the prison hulks in the Thames estuary after 1853, and men who had only served three years of a seven-year sentence could be released under this scheme. Ordinary folk started talking about all criminals as 'ticket of leave men'. The popular journals enjoyed creating this moral panic, making their readers envisage the local streets filling up with desperate and hardened criminals waiting to strangle them as they strolled to the Sunday band-stand concert.

All this led to the passing of the Garotter's Act of 1863. In some quarters people raised a glass to the villains because their actions had introduced extreme and repressive punishments back into the criminal law. In Bradford, the vogue had been just a small part of the life of a very violent and brutal community. One way of seeing this is to note that, while thugs were robbing in the dark streets, hundreds of men were gathering to watch bare-knuckle fighting, as they did at Cottingley Cliffs when Laverty and Curly fought on a Monday morning in this violent year. Two officers found the men fighting 'near the bottom of a small secluded nook near Cottingley Moor, the ground around rising up in the form of an amphitheatre'. There were six hundred people in the crowd, and the boxers were fighting for a prize of £10.

Everything about the city at this time suggests a community on the edge of reason and order; the women's refuge had hundreds of clients and even the traditional mummers' plays turned violent when fists flew on the doorsteps of good, honest people as the mummers' demands for cash grew too impertinent. There was even a minor scandal when some mill owners found themselves in the dock at the Borough Court. But at least there was no violence there: Thomas and Jeremiah Hall of Shipley had merely stolen £100 in a warehouse scam.

The year 1862 was a year of living dangerously in most English cities. In London street crime was obviously at a peak of atrocious violence, but the north was certainly not exempt from this 'new crime.' As so often, *Punch* saw the heart of the matter, and in their cartoon, 'Jones is not afraid of his shadow' they summed up the nature of this particular fear. The little man with top hat and umbrella sees the giant shadow of a garotter with a huge club on a wall as he walks along. But the good citizen in the picture, ironically, carries a revolver.

All Over a Bit o' Dripping

Sometimes, in the social history of the past, there have been kerfuffles over storms in tea-cups. In fact, there have been terrible battles over such things as, well – over dripping! There were times in the Victorian period when, in spite of the usual demands of the law and the innate sense of the importance of order and peace, the much distressed working class just found it too much to tolerate when an injustice was seen to be done.

In some cases it was about the price of corn; other disturbances were in response to the heavy hand of the law being used so heavily it has offended decency and reason. But then there were other causes of terrible acts of rebellion and destruction that stemmed from something very small – like dripping for instance. Dripping has long had a place in the Yorkshire cooking repertoire and older Leeds people will still talk fondly of their youth, when society was less health conscious and a treat was a dripping sandwich, salty, rich and satisfying. Back in 1865 dripping had dozens of uses for the woman of the house feeding her usually large family, and in the case of domestic servants, taking a little dripping from the cooking done for the employer was common practice and generally accepted. But not so in the household of Henry Chorley in Park Square. On this occasion, in February of that year, he refused to follow that common practice.

Eliza Stafford, fifty years old, was Chorley's cook and when she roasted a joint for him, she expected the dripping to take home. Chorley was a powerful man in the city: a magistrate and also a respected surgeon. But respect went out of the door on this occasion. It was when she was sent to Armley Gaol for the offence of taking the dripping that the trouble started. She was convicted of stealing two pounds of the stuff and given one month's imprisonment. She was quite new to his employment, having been there for only a few months, living in. When challenged about the matter she said that she was allowed it 'as a perquisite though I said nothing about that perquisite when I was first engaged to do the work.'

All hell broke out around Chorley's place. What had happened to make things worse was that her trial had been held in camera, and the Mayor of Leeds himself had been on the bench. The spark was lit, so to speak, by an article in a paper, as a report at the time noted:

> In a few days after the committal of the woman attention was called
> to the case, in a spirit of indignation, by one of the local papers which
> is best known for its publication of sensational stories and in its
> indulgence of caricature sketches of local personages …

The report also noted that newsboys were shouting out scraps of gossip and jokes, and that people were chatting about the affair in disgust; in the street this rhyme was heard:

> Now all you cooks and servant girls wot's very fond of tipping Don't
> take your master's scraps of fat and boil 'em down for dripping: for
> if you do bear this in mind, the magistrates won't fail to try you in
> a private court and send you off to gaol.

Time passed and then graffiti appeared on the walls of the Chorley home and on plenty of other walls, with such words as 'A month's imprisonment for 2lbs of dripping.' Then things escalated so that Chorley was vilified in the street and indeed harassed and bullied. He received threatening letters, and then placards began to appear expressing the view that Leeds people should assemble for a large celebration when Mrs Stafford came out of prison. But before that, pressure mounted. A large and aggressive crowd gathered outside Chorley's house. At first they shouted insults, and then they threw missiles at the house, including snowballs and stones. Chorley had the courage to come out and face them; he tried to talk to them and explain his position on the matter but to no avail. They threw dirt at him. When the police arrived they gradually dispersed, but there was worse to come.

Late in the evening on 22 February, a huge crowd assembled outside Armley Gaol expecting Mrs Stafford to appear, but she did not. The mob expected celebration but instead found that their friend was still locked up, or so they thought. In fact she had been let out earlier. After that the crowd were determined to go again to Chorley's house and this time they contrived to hang a bottle and an old dripping-pan to the end of a long pole. The police who stood by took a very long time to move the mob away.

Still the Leeds populace were not satisfied. The next day stones were thrown at the Chorleys' windows and the mob were pressing heavily on the forces of law. To make matters worse, the Chief Constable, Mr Bell, while trying to help move the crowd, fell heavily and dislocated a shoulder. The crowd mentality took over and when people fell they were crushed and trampled. One man was under the feet of the mob and was so seriously injured he had to be taken to the infirmary. The police could not cope.

The army at York were called for by telegraph, so by the evening men from the 8th Hussars were in Leeds and the authorities were not finished yet, because extra police from Bradford were called for as well. By 1865 the railways were well established and the soldiers travelled by train from York. There was a feeling of the riot being calmed by the time that the local journalists posted their reports but late that night a crowd of about 2000 gathered outside the town hall and shouted out insults. The police took the brunt of the anger as usual and as this mob was moved away, a stone cut deeply into the temple of one officer. There were several arrests, and that was inevitable given the scale of destruction and lawlessness that had filled the city like a rising tide of rage.

All this time, Mrs Stafford had been elsewhere. She had left Leeds much earlier, going to Scarborough where her daughter lived. The *Times* man reflected that she shown good sense 'preferring to avoid the questionable honours the crowd intended to confer upon her.' In other words, her appearance before her supporters would either have intensified the anger or made her a local hero. The politic action smacks of a reaction to sound advice from the police and prison Governor. In the end, it was decided that the five men arrested should not be dealt with seriously. There was perhaps a feeling of regret for the mean and thoughtless use of power by a bench of three influential men of high status, with one woman in front of them and the Chorleys and other witnesses trailing into the town hall to condemn her. The newspapers had imagined and recreated that scene in the eyes of the public, and the formula was one for extreme disorder on the streets of Leeds. We have to remember that the workers were one thing but the so-called 'underclass' were another matter. Usually when disorder hit the streets it was the lowest social order, desperate and pushed to the end of their tether by economic pressures such as the price of bread or the lack of jobs. But the Leeds dripping riots were, as far as we can gather, events in which decent people were goaded into militancy and sheer rage because of a terrible injustice against a decent working woman. In simple terms, it was a case of a confrontation between, on the one hand the practice of goodwill and convention ('perks of the job') and on the other hand the letter of the law. There was an element of absolute disgust at the immorality and injustice being shown by a man in high position. With hindsight, it is possible to say that the results of the street violence were partly a continuation of the old social convention of 'rough music' when a local wrongdoer was subject to torment and bullying for a moral 'crime' and also it was a case of total callousness on the part of a man who should have known better.

CHAPTER TWO
The Unexplained and Oddities

THERE IS SOMETHING in humans that longs for an unexplained experience, as we thrive on wonder, astonishment and mystery. As science has advanced over the centuries, so has the often undesirable element of explanation. There appears to be an explanation for everything, and the internet is peppered with people's stories and pictures of unexplained events. *The Fortean Times* continues to gather such tales, and that magazine engenders an attitude of informed interest. Science may have plenty of explanations for strange visions and experiences, but they are often merely theories, as tenable as any other, and in the end, those who see or feel paranormal happenings can do no more than trust their senses and explain the limits of their rational faculty. In numerous conversations on such topics, on countless occasions, I have heard people say, 'Well, there is no smoke without fire... and I know what I saw.'

Yorkshire, along with every other English county, has its paranormal history. Yet strangely, as I have found in various investigations in the county previously, there are 'hot spots' where more ghostly tales tend to gather than are seen as average. Some people reckon that these relate to 'ley lines' which are very ancient, and which, allegedly, provide focal points for the unexplained. In the late Victorian period, when the Society for Psychical Research was formed, ostensibly to undertake serious and scholarly research into paranormal phenomena, some of their most outstanding and intriguing cases were from Yorkshire, and I include one here, from Swanland near Hull. The other stories have been gathered from correspondents, and my acknowledgements to these writers are listed at the end of the book.

The Hand of Glory at the Spital Inn

In the eighteenth century, out on the wild moors between York and Carlisle, where the mail coach used to run, the ancient Spital Inn was a welcome little spot of comfort in a barren land. In early times, the place had been a hospital of sorts, as the name implies, and that had earlier been named as the *Rei Cross*, in Scots. The location was Stainmore – a name implying a stony, rough place, and so it was for the coaches, whose drivers knew the risks involved in travelling across that stretch of uneven and hard land.

In 1797 the Spital Inn was to become the site of one of Yorkshire's most harrowing occult tales. It hinges on the old belief that the severed hand of an executed felon, with a lit candle stuffed into the hand (a candle made of the corpse's lard), would have mystical and magical qualities.

In that year, the hostelry was run by George Alderson and his family, along with their servant, Bella. One autumn evening, George, his wife and their son, with Bella, had settled down, resting from the day's labours, and they had made all the right preparations to cope with the storm outside: they had built up a warm log-fire, drawn across the thick curtains, and barred the door. It was a wild, lawless land and a man's home had to be his special fastness against rogues as well as against the elements.

It had been a profitable day for the Aldersons as well: they had been to a fair at Brough Hill, and they had come away with a good stash of money, which had been stowed away in a bedroom cupboard. Consequently, there would have been a sense of ease and security on that wild night. The wind beyond the solid thick walls whistled and whipped the more fragile buildings outside; rain thrashed against the walls and the windows. Then, in the midst of this, came a knock at the door. There was a chain on the door, and Bella was told to open the door but keep the chain on. There before her stood an old woman, wrapped in a full cape and hood; she was drenched to the core and clearly suffered severely from the cold out in the storm. The family took pity and asked her in, then offered food and a bed for the night.

The old woman refused all this, and simply sat by the fire, keeping her coat and other clothes wrapped around her. She told the Aldersons that she had to leave early in the morning. Presently, off went the family to their beds, leaving Bella downstairs, and the girl started to make conversation with the old visitor. It was then that Bella saw something that alarmed her: looking at the old woman's leg on the fender, she saw a horseman's gaiters. In fact, the person was indeed a man, and she was filled with fear. Bella decided to pretend to be asleep, so she could watch the stranger out of one eye.

The figure then stood up, and there was a man, standing tall and strong. He took from his big pocket a withered human hand, then put a candle to it and lit it; then he stepped over to Bella, as her heart beat so strongly that she felt the pulse in her neck; he ran the candle close to her eyes to satisfy himself that she was asleep, and then he murmured,

> *Let those who rest more deeply sleep;*
> *Let those awake their vigils keep*

The figure than moved off, put the hand on the table and said,

> *Oh hand of glory, shed thy light:*
> *Show us to our spoil tonight.*

Then the figure moved again, going across to a window, where he pulled back a curtain, moved the candle-hand across, saying,

Flash out they light, oh skeleton hand
And show the way to our little band...

Finally, the stranger went to the door and unbarred it. A cutting wind came in from the freezing night, and the stranger whistled into the dark. Bella saw that there was no time to lose, and that there was serious trouble on the way if she didn't act fast. She got up, ran to the figure at the door and pushed it outside, then quickly barred the door again. Bella's problem now was to rouse the family. She ran upstairs and tried to wake them, as the door was being battered. But the charm had sent them into a deep sleep. What could she do?

Bella suddenly realised that the ghastly Hand of Glory was still down in the kitchen so she ran for it, and poured some water over the flame. As soon as the light was out, the family awoke. They heard the banging and shouting outside and George, along with his son, grabbed their firearms. George shouted at the band of robbers outside, commanding them to leave, but the villains called back that they wanted their booty and then they would leave the family in peace. George's son, upstairs, discharged his gun at the rogues outside and they took off.

The relief was palpable as the family safe inside the Spital Inn thanked God for their survival. Of course, they still possessed the withered hand, and the tale was passed on, that the family kept that grotesque memento for twenty years.

Hauntings at Home

Countless experiences of spectres seen within the confines of domestic life abound in the chronicles of haunting, and these are just a sample of such tales reported in a trawl for personal accounts of the unexplained around the county.

Amy Lofthouse recounts spirits in her family home: 'We lived in an end terrace house which was pretty old and we had creaky floorboards on the landing so you always heard if there was someone walking on them... My mum, my brother and I all experienced different things. My experience was always around the same time every night...' She recalls a typical visitation: someone walking across that landing. When her mother told her to get back to bed and to stop imagining things, it seemed a normal situation, but then, as Amy continues, 'My mother, who always has trouble sleeping, was up at about two or three in the morning... and I know she would not have made it up... the lights were off and she was just going back upstairs when she saw someone at the top of the stairs, looking down at her... she was so real that my mum actually said "get back to bed, it's early."'

Stairs and passages figure prominently in such sightings, and Julia Spearing, of Oakwood, has this tale: ' I was visiting my father and his wife one afternoon at their home in Oakwood. They had a little Yorkshire terrier who would run down the stairs into the hallway and trip people up... On this particular day, Sam tripped me up. Muttering under my breath, I continued up the stairs into the kitchen... there my step-mother was sitting, red-eyed and upset. She had just come back from the vet's, after having Sam put to sleep. Needless to say, I never mentioned my recent encounter!'

Joan Shaw was baby-sitting in West Bowling, Bradford, when she heard a noise downstairs. She thought it was her parents coming in, but as she says, 'I left my room and looked over the banister... when I saw that at the bottom of the staircase was a man looking up the stairs towards me. He then turned away and walked through the closed doors and into the front room. The odd thing is really that there was no light on those stairs and yet I could see clearly.' Once again, we have stairs involved.

Churwell Scrap-Yard

Jade McGlynn has recalled a powerful experience from the location of Churwell, a village nestled between Leeds and Morley. She wrote that there had been lots of reports of strange sightings around the scrap-yard and old mining site which are at the bottom of Churwell Hill. A typical unexplained tale is this:

> *One day an old woman was coming up the path. She stopped and talked to Jack and told him that she lived in the house opposite the scrap-yard when she was a child...*
>
> *She asked Jack if anything unusual had happened at the yard or in a white cottage nearby, and when Jack said yes, she said that as a child she would see ghosts of miners travelling up the path and past her house...*
>
> *The lady said her mother had told her there had been a mining disaster at the pit shaft and that many men had died and their bodies had never been retrieved...*

This may refer to the Morley Main accident of 1872, when several men from Churwell and Gildersome died.

The scrap-yard appears to be some kind of epicentre of activity, as Jade has recounted several tales relating to the area, including a sighting of part of a man 'in a wall' – something with which ghost-hunters are familiar, as if a time-slip has offered a vision of life existing at a level previous to the current one when the sighting is made. She has been meticulous in keeping records of sightings and reports. It does appear to be a significantly atmospheric spot.

The Strange White Figure at Hebden Bridge

Some years ago, after my collection of paranormal Yorkshire tales was publlished, I appealed for more from readers, and Philip Bolton wrote to let me know about his experience with a signalman at Hebden Bridge. Most readers of Charles Dickens know about his famous short story, *The Signalman*, but Philip's is a close rival when it comes to fear on the tracks. Around forty years ago he was working as a signalman and he was on the Sunday Night shift. After eleven at night there was little to do until the next train, which passed after six hours of silence.

Philip was only in his twenties when this happened, and he recalls that some of the older workmen tended to drop off to sleep in this long stretch of time. But Philip did not. He used the time well, including learning to play on the banjo. But then, on one particular shift, he dimmed the lights and sat, enjoying a smoke with his pipe.

But then he looked out, to the left and he saw, as he puts it, 'a brilliant white figure walking down the platform outside my box... for a second it vanished but then reappeared at the top of the stairs, came through the closed door... and stood by my side.' He jumped to his feet, reached for the light-switch and turned the light on. He adds, 'To say I needed the toilet is an understatement.' He replayed that scene in his mind, over and over. Had he dreamt it? We are bound to ask that question. But then, he was not the only one, and in studying the paranormal, we always want the verification of a second sighting. Philip had exactly that.

He notes that another signalman, working the same shift, had made the effort to let lots of people know: he rang the other men in the boxes on the circuit and also rang the police. That left him open to some teasing, as he had to go through the experience and make it sound convincing. Although there was some humour, the fact is that the man resigned: he left at six the next morning and never came back to his work. Philip concludes his tale with the observation that it had to be a bad experience for a young man with a wife and children to walk out on well-paid employment. Did the two men see the same thing? It seems more than likely so.

The Swanland Poltergeist

In the village of Swanland, a few miles west of Hull, there was a joiner's shop, and this was to be the site of strange events, so we must begin with a description of the place, as supplied by a Mr Bristow, who worked his apprenticeship there: 'It was of one storey, about 10 feet high, with three slender tie-beams placed across at intervals, and was quite open to the roof, its length being about 40 feet and its width 17 or 18 feet... The building was quite detached, being bounded on one side by a country road, whilst the other... faced a grass field. Down the centre were arranged two joiners' benches, which, placed end to end, extended about half the length of the shop.'

Mr Bristow told an investigator, Professor Sidgwick, that from his workbench he could see the other two joiners, and the disturbances began one day when one of these men was startled and said, 'You fellows had better keep your pieces of wood to yourselves and get on with your work.' When he was asked what he was talking about he replied, 'You know very well what I mean... one of you has pelted this piece of wood at me.' He showed the wood, and both men working with him denied having thrown it.

There followed more scraps of wood, aimed at and hitting, the complainant; Mr Bristow then pointed out to the other two that he had not been hit, and that prompted a piece of wood to hit him quite hard in his ribs. The three men stopped and had a chat about what had just happened. Mr Bristow was detailed to climb a ladder and see what could be seen up above. This is what he reported:

As I was descending, and my head being on a level with one of the beams, a piece of wood, about the size of two fingers, came dancing along, taking about two feet at a bound, making a full stop about at my ear... I said to my companions in bewilderment, 'There is

something more than a trick in this...'
One of them agreed with me. The other maintained it was only
a clever trick being played upon us somehow...

Following that, another piece of wood came hurtling towards the other two, and one of the men, who was wearing a silk hat, had it knocked off his head. This kind of activity went on for some time, with more and more scraps of wood being thrown. Then the foreman arrived, and this man, brimming with rationality and common sense, scoffed at the whole business, but as he stopped talking, as Mr Bristow recalled, '... a piece with a somewhat sharp point came dashing from a distant part of the roof and stuck into the board betwixt our fingers.' The foreman 'stood aghast'

One of the most energetic and respected investigators of the Society for Psychical Research, a man called Myers, went to study the phenomenon. When he met Bristow he heard the story that the son of one of the partners in the business, a man called John Gray, had died of consumption while being a worker there. Apparently, John Gray had insisted that his uncle, William Habbershaw, pay off creditors who were troubling Mr Gray senior. According to Bristow, this uncle once took him on a job some miles from the workshop, and 'he began to talk to me about the phenomena as if he wished to get me to put them down to some natural cause. His manner was that of a man almost petrified with terror. I felt convinced that he had had disturbances of which we knew nothing.' It seems that the money was paid and the troubles stopped.

Unusually for such investigations, some later visits were made by Society members to see some of the workers in Swanland who might recall these strange events, and a few were interviewed. Interestingly one Thomas Andrews, who was the man whose hat was knocked off by a wood splinter, was found, and one investigator wrote this:

To illustrate this [the unusual force of the wood] he made us hold his
stick and showed how a piece would come along and go round the
stick, as it were, and he said, 'No-one could throw like that...

The events were investigated by members of the Society for Psychical Research and a full report was written. There is no doubt that the whole affair was taken seriously by the scientifically-minded investigators of the time.

A Pub Haunting

Unusually, in this story, the names used are false, as there is a need for privacy. It is the tale of a haunting and an exorcism regarding a public house in the West Riding, close to the M62 motorway. It happened back in 1974, and the vicar involved wrote a detailed report of the terrifying events. He put these words on the first page of his report:

My own simple experience of this matter is that I have been confronted
by four people who are normally healthy, happy, sane and intelligent,
and who have been reduced to a state of absolute terror.

It all began when the vicar was visited by Harry and Derek, who were nervous and reticent at first, wondering what the attitude of a churchman would be to a ghost story. But this was soon to be nothing remotely resembling a problem, as the man of the cloth was open-minded and receptive.

Harry and Derek, with their wives Pauline and Sue, and their children, had stayed at the Belford Inn while the landlady was away. From the beginning there were unsettling experiences, as the report summarises:

The first night Pauline had heard a rustling sound. Derek had not,
though. Both had heard a banging noise which seemed to come from

a long passage. Outside their bedroom. The following night the bangings and rustlings continued... they were frightened. The next day they asked Harry and Sue to stay with them... they went around the house wedging beer-mats into windows, doors, etc., to stop any possible sources... but still the rustling and banging continued. They said it sounded like footsteps running backwards and forwards in the passage, yet the house was empty except for themselves...

After this, both couples and the children all slept in the one room, for security; but worse was to follow. Derek and Harry heard noises which seemed to be from an intruder, so, as the report goes on, 'They were amazed to look up and down the passage and see no-one. It was then, said Derek, that the "thing" got him. He said it seemed to come at him from the top corner of the passage with a loud hissing and crackling sound. He felt himself enveloped by some invisible force.'

He screamed out that they should all get out fast, and Harry had a decision to make: did he follow Derek or should he retreat back into the bedroom and cower there? He rushed forward and both men made a break. As the vicar's report noted, 'they arrived at the bottom of the stairs, Harry on Derek's back.'

The vicar had been approached because the family wanted him to conduct an exorcism. This all happened in a parish other than his own; he needed his Bishop's permission, and hence the written report. It went ahead; after all, the appeal to the vicar had come after words had been written on a mirror: I WILL KILL YOU.

The rite of exorcism took place. People stood in a circle and the vicar held a crucifix in his right hand and a bottle of holy water in his left; he spoke the words of the rite. He then walked slowly to each room, and finally to the living room where prayers were completed. He told the family that the spirit would leave them.

It worked. The vicar's report ends with the words: 'The family are convinced that their ghost is gone. They no longer sense the evil presence.'

The Freak Weather of 1844 and Frogs from Heaven

In the twenty-first century we are becoming accustomed to floods and storms of more than usual intensity. But these are not new occurrences. In 1844 across Yorkshire we had some of the most bizarre weather on record. The thunderstorm was notably violent around Leeds and towards the Humber. Leeds itself was wrapped in darkness in the early afternoon of the 24 June. A carrier travelling to Leeds from Pateley Bridge had one horse killed and the other injured; in Bramley a chimney was thrown down to the earth. Horsforth saw trees split and a cow belonging to a Mr Stansfield killed.

> *The sufferings of livestock were enumerated by the local chroniclers: 'The storm did much damage at Huddersfield, flooding the streets in the Lower part of the town four or five feet deep. At Halifax the streets in a Line with Gibbet Street and Crow Street were covered with a broad stream Of considerable depth. At Billingley near Barnsley Mr Micklethwaite had a mare And foal killed. A calf and sheep belonging to Mr Russell, of Hoyland, were killed...'*

But then came the strangest report: 'At Selby, with the fall of the rain, there was a shower of frogs. Several were caught in their descent by holding out hats for that purpose. They were about the size of a horse-bean and remarkably lively after their aerial but wingless flight...'

The Map of Wales at Yordas Cave

The caves of Ingleton have long fascinated Yorkshire folk and of course, the thousands of visitors who visit this magical place every year. In any tourist publication on the county, one would find mention of Ingleborough, Whernside, Pen y Ghent and Gragareth. The Celtic names themselves suggest something alien, something reaching back far into the mists of time, and indeed this topography does that. There is staggering beauty in the caves, fells and falls of the area. As one writer, John Hamer, noted, back in the 1940s, describing Lost John's Cave, 'Where a wall runs down from Gragareth and crosses the allotment road close to a sheep-pen... lies hidden one of the most stupendous and lofty caverns in England.'

But if we leave aside the attractions of the landscape and of the inner chasms of this daunting country, we have an instance of one of those peculiar and attractive features of geomorphology – the incidental shaping of a feature which is a bizarre sight for the visitor who comes upon it by surprise. This is at Yordas Cave in Kingsdale: in 1751, this was described by Richard Pococke as 'a very grand, high cave' and William Wordsworth went there in 1800, including mention of it in his great poem, *The Prelude.* The place became a show cave later. This feature is no less than a weird shape which looks almost exactly like the outline of a map of Wales.

The cave is composed of Lower Carboniferous limestone and the beck, called Yordas, runs through it, forming a waterfall called Chapter House, and then the stream is seen again at the Kingsdale Master Cave. One might expect the cave to have a certain disturbing atmosphere because, as John Hutton, writing in the 1780s noted, back in 1730 a young woman who was travelling by herself, in spite of being pregnant, took refuge in the place but died there.

The outline made by the rock is clear in a photo taken by H. W. Rhodes in the 1940s.

The cave stone shaped like the outline of Wales

CHAPTER THREE

Nowt so Queer as Folk: Characters

T HE PHRASE AT the head of this chapter originated in Yorkshire. It suggests a real curiosity about people, and that can range from nosiness to insult, often borne of misunderstanding. But actually, experience shows that what really lies behind this old saying is a tolerance of others. Yorkshire loves its eccentrics largely because they illustrate the possibility of going it alone, going one's own way, being true to the self, however odd and non-conformist. The characters in this chapter all show these qualities in different ways.

In my experience of growing up in Yorkshire, I must record that yes, there was always an abundance of people with character, and not a few who could be confidently termed eccentric or odd, but this was often said as a compliment to their creativity. After all, the celebrities of recent times have proved this to be the case, when we look at such outstanding personalities in the media as Michael Parkinson, Ian MacMillan, Hannah Hauxwell, Gervase Phinn and of course, Alan Bennett.

Most Yorkshire autobiographies have 'characters' as central figures, and perhaps such types were in the past generated by the deep need that Tykes have for being left alone, being allowed to grow in their own way and being tolerated in spite of odd habits and the occasional unhealthy preoccupation with some kind of hobby, the latter not always what the stereotype suggests: such things as pigeons and greyhounds. No, there is a dogged individuality about traditionally-made Yorkshire folk.

A Hero of Dettingen

The Battle of Dettingen was fought in 1743 during the War of the Austrian Succession, and in that confrontation, a joint force of British and Hanoverian men faced a French army of 70,000 under Marshall Maurice. The French came off worst, but losses were heavy on both sides. It was a major battle, and its story has often been told, but as with all large-scale events, there are footnotes, and one of the Dettingen footnotes concerns a Yorkshireman called Thomas Brown.

Brown was a private in Brigadeer Bland's regiment of Dragoons. He was born at Kirkleatham in the North Riding, and he was to win, as one Victorian writer, James Caulfield put it, 'the applause and approbation, not only of his own comrades and officers, but likewise the unqualified praise of the whole army.' In the early phase of the engagement, he had been in the thick of the struggle and two horses had been shot under him before his first severe wound was sustained – two fingers of one had were chopped off. But then, his real valour was to show itself.

Caulfield describes what happened when he determined to regain the captured standard of his regiment: '... he was necessitated to make his way through a lane of the enemy, exposed to the fire and sword of those who had witnessed the destruction of their own *gens d'armes*. And notwithstanding the most vigorous resistance of the enemy to stay him in his progress, he succeeded in bearing away his prize, at the expense of eight cuts in the face, head and neck; and two musket balls in his back; independent of these... he had three balls pass through his hat.... and was hailed on his safe arrival with the standard, by three distinct huzzas...'

When he did this amazing feat of courage, Brown was just twenty-eight. Unfortunately, his image has come down to posterity in the shape of a portrait showing the disfigurements of his face after that retrieval of the colours. In the Victorian publication, *Old Yorkshire*, his picture is reproduced, showing him in uniform, with a huge scar down his forehead, a cracked nose and another scar across his upper lip. Yet he still looks sturdy enough and very dignified.

What was his reward? If there had been a Victoria Cross, then surely he would have won it, but he had to settle for 'a liberal pension of a shilling a day, to pass the remnant of his life in luxurious ease and enjoyment' as Caulfield puts it. One suspects that such a personality would never have been satisfied with a life simply watching the vegetables grow.

Thomas Brown,
the hero of Dettingen
Old Yorkshire journal, 1880

Owd Joe of Ingleton

In Anthony Hewitson's memoirs of Ingleton, dealing with the 1840s, there is an account of a man who may stand in place as the representative and epitome of a certain Yorkie type: one who loves his drink and is a loner but who, as Hewitson put it, 'is a sort of genius.'

Owd Joe was Joseph Yeadon, and Hewitson sums him up with these words:

> *He was a first-rate mechanic; he had also a barometric faculty and in other departments he was skilful. He once actually built a house – dressed, or got ready the stones for it and prepared the timber. He virtually put together and completed the whole structure with his own hands; and this building in which he lived for some time is still standing [in the 1890s] it forms part of a business store...*

But there was something else about him – and here lies his eccentricity. He put on an act, or a 'front' and this was a ruse to pretend to the world that, if he were entering a public house, it was not with any view to settle and sink more drinks than might be polite and workmanlike. With that ruse in mind, he always carried tools with him. As Hewitson adds, ' Sometimes, when not too far gone, he would on leaving take away with him the article he brought in but it was oftener left than taken.'

In other villages throughout the county there have been such characters noted, like the man who always had a worker's dark overall on, and an oil-rag in one hand, while all the time he was sinking pints. Then there was the plumber from a village I once knew who described jobs he had done up and down the county, speaking as if he had rightfully retired from his trade, yet he was only thirty years old.

But Joe's front was always known by the Ingleton locals. Hewitson ends with this: 'One day he was seen walking or stepping into a public house

with an ash grate on his shoulder. An old native who noticed this, and knew his ways, shortly afterwards said... "Well now, Owd Joe surely must have got to the far end." Perhaps he had, though nobody could really tell for certain.'

What the tale does illustrate is the Yorkie's love of a drama, a show, a 'reet good turn' which will entertain and baffle. I think Joe took some pleasure in his little act.

The inn where Owd Joe enjoyed a drink Hewitson's Autobiography

58

Tight is Not the Word!

Yes, of course, when people think of stereotype Tykes they lump them alongside the Scots and try to insist that they are miserly by nature. All generalisations are wrong and sometimes offensive, but it has to be said that in days long gone, the county did have some extreme examples of those men whose wallets gather cobwebs and whose mattresses hid a stash of notes. Such a one was John Turner, born in Ripon but who moved to Bradford for his adult life, where he won a reputation for being a man whose temperament would have made Scrooge look like a spendthrift.

Turner's family were farmers, but when he came to Bradford he worked in a shop run by a Mr Sayer, and later he took over the business, which was by the Bowling Green inn, and in fact Turner raised enough cash to buy the property, and he never looked back. He launched himself into a life of parsimony and absolute basic living costs, even dispensing with any finery he had; apparently he set out to devote himself entirely to massing funds and wealth. As one contemporary writer explained, '... so firmly had he disciplined mind and body that for some years he took only a few hours to sleep amongst the piles of goods with which his place was packed from basement to attic. His journeys to Manchester he performed on foot, or occasionally got a lift on a carrier's wagon, but whether he paid for the ride is doubtful, as parting with money was for him one of life's cardinal sins.'

One of his favourite habits was to approach the travelling men, those who covered hundreds of miles with their wares on their backs, at the end of their journeys, when they were desperate to sell leftovers. Doing this, he would ensure a maximum profit on his sales of course. When he finally had enough of the business, according to a writer in *Old Yorkshire* magazine, he walked off with £16,000 and in today's values we would have to multiply that by around 60. But having ceased trading, and moved to Starbeck near Harrogate, he did not choose to spend and be happy in a life of material wealth. No, he continued in his miserly ways; he still earned and saved. One account notes that ' Here, secluded in his own house, in the privacy of his own grounds... did the Bradford draper accumulate with greater eagerness than before. Nothing that would realise money escaped his cold, grey eyes. But there were instances of his greed for wealth causing him pains and problems, such as the time he travelled to Ripon to collect a debt, and for this he accepted a grindstone. He then took it from its frame and tried to wheel it home, but the thing broke in two not so far from his home.

The date of his death is not known exactly, but it was probably around 1875, as one writer writing in 1882 notes that Turner died 'six years or so ago.' He died in Harrogate, aged eighty-one. But he had not been entirely alone: he married and had a son, and he bragged that in married life his annual spending was only around £20. If we needed to show one image of him that summed up his parsimony, it would be the tale told by a man who met him as they both walked across the wilds of Rombalds Moor. Turner was bare-footed, carrying his shoes tied together and slung over his shoulder, to save the wear and tear on their soles.

Mr Tit Bits

The popular magazine, *Tit Bits*, was the brainchild of George Newnes, who was the doyen of popular print media for the late Victorian and Edwardian years; it ran from 1881 to 1989 in various forms, and its contributors in the early days included Rider Haggard and P.G.

The Leeds man who became a walking advert The Strand magazine

60

Wodehouse. It published popular fiction, ran competitions, and had almost every category of material we might think of in weekly magazines today. In the 1890s, it was so enterprising that it encouraged rather experimental forms of advertising and a number of gimmicks – fashions that were later to be fully exploited by the rogue Horatio Bottomley.

In 1896, *Tit Bits* found its ideal promoter, and this was in the shape of that fascinating creature, the Yorkie eccentric. In this case it was James Wilson, of Farsley. James entered any competition he could, dressed as Mr Tit Bits. This meant that he rode a bike, and his attire was composed entirely of cut-out parts of the magazine. Thus he had a cone-shaped hat, long jacket, ruff and pantaloons all made from cuttings. He started his remarkable career by entering a Stanningley competition at the carnival, in which he was up against fifty other entrants, all riding bicycles. He was hard to miss, so gaudy was the impact of his appearance: even the spokes of his bike were covered with sheets of the magazine.

James then won prizes at similar events held at Eccleshill, Wibsey Park and Leeds. On one occasion he won first prize in a fund-raising event at Leeds, supporting medical charities. Fame soon followed, and he found himself pictured in *The Strand* magazine, alongside such characters as the Spencer Brothers and their balloon, and the Indian Prince and his Hunting Cheetah.

A Genius from Halifax and Another from Leeds

Sometimes the unusual in a person's character is not eccentric, nor queer in any way, but is, in fact, a quality that could only be called genius. That surely applies to Percy Shaw, born in Halifax in 1890. He started out in life doing labouring work, but then did what so many autodidacts have done: he went to evening classes and worked for an education, acquiring shorthand skills and accounting; but he also had a very practical, capable turn of mind, and there were surely signs of his future achievement when he joined Mr Shaw Senior in setting up a repair firm for lawnmowers.

Percy was destined to be an inventor, and in that line of work, he went beyond mere repairs, to the invention of a miniature motor roller. Now, not long after, he set about inventing some kind of remedy for the problems caused by foggy roads. Driving around the hilly and undulating Calder Valley in a mist was a particularly dangerous, and especially so when there were no markings on the road. Seeing that headlights made signs clear, he got to work devising some kind of light-source – something that would utilise the car headlights. The result was the cats' eyes studs now so familiar on our roads. But did he actually get the inspiration from seeing cats' eyes? The unofficial record says so. Whether that is a myth or not, who knows?

But the cats' eyes were patented in 1934 and Percy formed a company to make them – the Reflecting Road-studs Company. Then, thirteen years later, they were officially ordered and applied across the land. When Ken Dodd delivers his almost endless comedy show, he often slots in his little joke about what Percy might have done had the backsides of cats been his inspiration, rather than the eyes. Doddy comments that if so, Percy would have invented the pencil-sharpener.

Whatever the inspiration, the result was a revolution – and it saved countless lives, one would argue, over the years since Percy's brainwave.

Jimi Heselden makes an interesting comparison. In fact, I was at school with him. We were both born in 1948, and he was five months older than I. We both left school when we were fifteen, but Jimi was a much rarer and very enterprising individual. On leaving school he worked as a labourer in a colliery, and when he was made redundant, he used the money to rent a workshop. The rest is history. Here is the man who invented the now ubiquitous Hesco bastion barrier system, which uses a collapsible defence or stronghold barrier. This is now seen everywhere, with military and civil engineering applications.

Jimi was a kind, thoughtful man, and the manner of his death, in 2010, says a great deal about him. He had bought the Segway Company and was making a great deal of money when one day, riding a segway near Leeds, he stopped to allow a walker to pass, as they were on a cliff. Jimi lost control and fell over the edge. He died from the fall. This was the man who gave large donations to the Help for Heroes fund and other good causes. He left a huge sum of money at his death, but all this is immaterial really.

The point about Jimi Heselden is that he was a gentleman, and he had that nose for business that characterises the Yorkshire spirit. He and Percy Shaw were two of a kind, and their contributions to modern life have been massive. They also prove that originality and creativity come from sheer observation and self-belief, or, as it might be said in the county, 'they nivver missed a trick.'

Poor Bill Sharp

Back in the middle years of Victoria's reign, a few miles from Keighley, a man called William Sharp once found the woman whom he wanted to be his wife. The wedding was arranged, but the girl's parents did not approve and they kept her at home. That was as far as William went in his life, because from that day on, he lived in a small house, nine feet square, with a bed, a table and an open fire. He acquired the name of 'Old Three Laps' and became one of the county's most strange characters, never leaving that tiny home until his death in March, 1856.

William had his window fastened down and the lower panes boarded over to keep out prying eyes. He lived a life in retreat, like a true hermit. His father saw that he had food, and that was all he needed. One writer working not long after William's death wrote about the man's eating habits:

In this bed and unventilated nook he remained for thirty-eight years, obstinately refusing to speak even to his constant attendant, and forbidding anyone else to enter the room... He did ample justice to the food procured for him, and became excessively stout. His flesh was thick and firm, and his estimated weight was about 240 pounds. He ate his meals in a curious way, for his legs became contracted and drawn up towards his body, and when about to eat his food he used to roll himself over, and so take his meals in a kneeling posture, and to prevent any crumbs getting into the blankets on which he lay...'

The coffin used for him was massive, being around 480 pounds in weight when his body was in it. Strangely, this coffin was made in the room, and so when it had to be moved, some of the wall had to be knocked down to allow the funeral to take place.

William, when in decline, was heard to utter, 'Poor Bill, poor Bill... poor Bill Sharp!'

Fletcher Christian's Descendant Saved by Venom

In 1938 Sheffield was the scene of a remarkable piece of hospital life-saving when Walter Woodbine from Walkley was close to death, choking and fighting for breath. The man was a haemophilia sufferer, and of course, he was bleeding to death and blood was filling up in his throat. This happened after he fell from a ladder and bit his tongue.

His tongue became swollen, and the substance of the tongue, together with the flowing blood, blocked his windpipe. He was rushed to hospital, and smart medic saw that the answer to the problem was to apply some venom from a viper. This was put on the tip of his tongue, and the bleeding began to cease.

Some days after, the man was still struggling to speak or eat, and only by the application of icy water could his health be maintained until time healed the wounds. For people without haemophilia, the venom would be fatal, but the reason for this is that the venom causes clotting – exactly what Mr Woodbine needed for his life to be saved.

The newspapers picked up the detail that the man was descended from the famous mutineer against Captain Bligh on the *Bounty*: Fletcher Christian, played memorably by Marlon Brando in the Hollywood version of the story.

Great Silences

Keeping quiet for any length of time takes a lot of doing. There have to be exceptional reasons for people not to use their vocal organs for periods extending over years. But these two tales illustrate some of the extremes in this context. First there is the story of Mrs Emily Bibby and her son John, from 1939.

Mrs Bibby found herself in the coroner's court when the inquest on her seventeen-year-old son John was held. It was not only a sad occasion, but a remarkable one too. This was because young John had never spoken since he was born. For all those years in which mother and son had been together, she had masticated his food and fed him, as one report put it, 'just like a bird.' John had died from asphyxia in hospital, and poor Emily, who was married to a lighterman, said that her son was her 'heart and soul.'

Since his birth, the little boy had never been physically able to chew any food. Mrs Bibby did what nature necessitated: she chewed food for him until it was manageable for him to manipulate in his little mouth. But then, when his mother was so poorly that she had to be taken to hospital, the boy died. Naturally, such a mode of life interested the medical experts, and in a press report from the time, one authority was quoted as saying, 'It is not unique for a boy of the type mentioned to be kept alive under hospital conditions, where there are special means of feeding the patient, but it is unusual for such a case to reach the age of seventeen.'

The coroner's verdict was 'death by misadventure.' We can only try to imagine the mother's staggering devotion to her duties and to her profound love, in doing what she did for so long.

The other tale reads like such a simple, uncomplicated statement of a killing: ' York Assizes: Abraham Bairstan, aged sixty, was put to the bar, charged with the wilful murder of Sarah Bairstan his wife, in the parish of Bradford.' In the busy, overworked courts of the Regency, dealing with new and often puzzling crimes form the labouring classes in the fast-growing towns, it was maybe just another 'domestic' that went too far. But this is far from the truth, and the Bairstan case gives us an insight into the plight of those unfortunate people at the time who were victims of ignorance as well as of illness. In this instance it was an awful, anguished mental illness that played a major part in this murder.

When the turnkey brought Bairstan into the court he commented that he had not heard the prisoner say a word since he was brought to York and locked up. This was nothing new to the man's family. Mr Baron Hullock, presiding, was shocked but also full of that natural curiosity of someone who just does not understand something. He pressed the gaoler to explain. He asked if the man in the dock understood the spoken word, and the answer was no. He also ascertained that Bairstan appeared to have no response to any sound whatsoever, nor any movement. It makes painful reading in the court report to note that the prisoner was a 'dull and heavy looking man who… cast a vacant glance around the court.' The reporter in 1824 noted that the man 'appeared totally insensible of the nature of the proceedings.'

Poor Hullock had a real challenge to try to communicate with the man, trying his best to make the prisoner make any sound at all, asking several questions but receiving no answer. When he asked 'Do you hear what I say to you?' Bairstan simply stared at the officer next to him.

It was obviously going to be one of those trials at which many people were thinking that this silence was the best ruse if a man wanted to avoid the rope. The judge had to instruct the jury about potential fraud and the possibility that this was a tough and amoral killer with a canny wit and impressive acting skills. In legal jargon, the point was, was the man standing there fraudulently, wilfully and obstinately, or 'by the act and providence of God?' It was going to be a hard task, one might think, but not so: enter his sons and a close friend. They told a very sad story, and an astounding one, given that Bairstan managed to marry and raise a family.

His friend stated that he had known the prisoner for over fifty years, and that he was sure that ten years had passed since Bairstan had fallen silent. He explained that his two sons had been looking after the old man in that time. His key statement was that 'while he was sane, his wife and he had lived together very comfortably.' The man, Jeremiah Hailey, added that his friend had been capable of merely saying yes or no, and that the last time he had heard the man speak was when he had asked him if he knew his friend Jeremiah. 'He said aye, but I think he did not know me.'

Bairstan's two sons confirmed that their father had been silent in that ten-year period, only excepting one or two words. Henry said that since being locked up, his father had been pressed to speak and had answered something sounding like. 'Be quiet... be quiet'. The other son, Joseph, confirmed that his father had been 'out of his mind' for ten years. There had been enough in him to marry and earn a living, but we must see with hindsight and more relevant knowledge, that Abraham Bairstan had been struck by a paralysis, perhaps combined with a depressive mental illness. In 1824, the most meaningful explanation was to put it down to God's will, so the jury found that the prisoner stood mute 'by the visitation of God.'

The Prophet Wroe

In the 1830s crowds would gather around Tyrrel Street and Bridge Street to listen to a preacher, but the speaker in question was nothing to do with any orthodox faith. He was the prophet John Roe, who was born in Bowling in 1782, and whose home was still standing in the 1890s when Bradford historian William Scruton wrote about him. Scruton pointed out that Wroe also used an upstairs room in the old Cock Pit to hold a service, but more striking was his journey into town:

> ...to this place he walked in procession with twelve virgins dressed in white and with long white falls. The prophet himself was conspicuous by the flowing beard and brown hat worn by the 'faithful.' The large crowds that assembled were generally of a peaceful sort, and did nothing more than indulge in a bit of pleasant banter, but it was when the prophet challenged his audience within the walls of the Cock Pit to a discussion on the merits of South-cottianism that the peace was broken and the temperature suddenly changed from calm to stormy.

The creed in question, Southcottianism, refers to the thought of Joanna Southcott, (1750-1814) who was a farmer's daughter with a penchant for the supernatural. She claimed to be the woman in the Apocalypse and foretold the birth of a new Messiah, giving the exact date of his birth. This did not happen, but nothing moved her faith in her beliefs. She left a box with items of supposed importance regarding her prophecies, and this was eventually opened in 1927 by the famous ghost-hunter, Harry Price. There was nothing of real interest, but strangely, the items included a pistol and a lottery ticket.

Whatever Southcott's messages may have been to her contemporaries, her personality certainly had a marked effect on Mr Wroe. It appears that he was married, and then not long after that he was seriously ill, and his return to health was marked by some kind of feverish insistence that he saw visions. As Scruton observed, 'Little wonder that he should conceive the idea that he was singled out by God for the purpose of carrying on some great mission on earth.'

Hence we have the procession of Wroe on his donkey, followed by the lines of virgins. As with Yorkshire's more celebrated prophet, Mother Shipton of Knaresborough, Wroe made prophecies. At Southcott's death, there had been no Redeemer, no new Messiah, and of course, Wroe saw for himself that very role, awaiting his genius. Such a character was bound to attract critics and opponents, and naturally some appeared, including John Rushton, who had pamphlets and broadsides printed attacking the Southcottians. Typical of his language is this:

Mr Wroe the Southcottian
Scruton's *Pen and Pencil Sketches of Old Bradford*

Have you been at the theatre at Darley Street top?
Which wise men all pass by; where fools love to stop;
Where zealots hold forth, and make whimsical speeches
About some old woman that makes up old breeches.

Waterton, Crocodile Rider

The essayist and biographer, E.V. Lucas, writing in 1930, was well aware of the strange attraction one feels towards the life of a truly lovable eccentric. For Lucas, this was Charles Waterton. Lucas wrote, that Waterton was a wanderer: ' He began in 1802, at the age of twenty when he went to Cadiz and witnessed the ravages of the plague of Malaga. In 1804 he sailed for British Guiana; in 1812 he was in Brazil; in 1816 he was in Pernambuco, and in 1817 he was in Rome, where he climbed to the top of the lightning conductor of St Peter's and stood on the head of the angel on the Castello. It was in Demerara in 1820 that he performed his great feat of riding on a cayman, which all students of crossword-puzzles know to be a crocodile...'

But then he settled down to life in Walton Hall, Wakefield, where he had been born in 1782. His family tree included Sir Thomas More, and indeed he was a staunch Catholic. The roots of his family lie in Lincolnshire, where they were once Lords of the Manor of Waterton, but after various legal transactions, the family became settled in Yorkshire, and a Victorian account of the family seat, Walton Hall, gives a very vivid impression of the place:

> *The old family house, built a thousand years ago [the author wrote in 1880] was a fine castellated building, with a noble wainscoted hall, 90 feet long, where the Watertons for many centuries banqueted with their friends and drunk the health of Philip and Mary, the Charleses and Jameses, and the 'King over the water'... Becoming decayed, it was taken down by Charles Waterton's father, who built the existing ugly mansion in its place, leaving only... a picturesque old gateway...*

In this seat, Waterton settled down after his extensive travels, and had plenty of experience to write about in his new, more sedentary life. One typical adventure is this, described by Frederick Ross: '... he was passing down a river in a canoe when he saw a huge Laboris snake – a powerful and deadly poisonous creature – on the bank. He wounded it with a gunshot, and caused the canoe to be brought up to the bank in order to secure the specimen. He laid hold of the branch and was preparing to grasp it by the throat, when the tillerman turned the boat off and left Waterton swinging from the branch, half in the water... thrice going overhead in the river, which was swarming with caymen...'

Back home, arguably his most impressive achievement was his creation of a bird sanctuary. He had a high wall built around the land, and to pay for that he stopped drinking his favourite wine; inside that sanctuary, he ordered, nothing must be killed. No keepers with dogs were allowed to tread in that place and as Lucas noted, Nature preserves the balance.

Inside the Hall, there was a museum. Lucas explains how this fitted in with Waterton's passions: 'Taxidermy was indeed his secondary pleasure in life, observing being the first... HE slept in the room where he worked, extending himself on the bare boards, in a single blanket, with a block of oak for a pillow. ' His Catholic regime included a midnight visit to his chapel and as Lucas notes, 'After an hour or so more sleep he rose promptly at three o'clock, lit his fire and then lay down for half an hour's wakeful meditation, which time he called his half hour of luxury.' One story that sums up his eccentricity and also his charm is that of his carrying a knife with him everywhere, and on one occasion he met a tramp, who begged the knife of him. He told the tramp to take the knife to a certain cobbler in Wakefield, and if he did that, the cobbler would supply the tramp with new boots. It all worked out as planned.

Ironically, he died after a fall in his own park at home, in 1865. The story goes that when Waterton lay dying, the Pope telegraphed a blessing. There is something about Waterton's life and quirks that remind us just how important it is to allow individuals and adventurers to have some scope, to be themselves. Without the Watertons, the world would be a very dull place. E.V. Lucas, who wrote on thousands of everyday topics in his long writing life, singled out the Yorkshire traveller for special attention, as he represents a very rare thing: the person who has no shame or self-consciousness, but just 'goes for it.'

Blind Jimmy and Tommy Ramsden

Blind Jimmy was the nick-name of a certain James Mortimer. He was basically a drifter, but there is no record of his actually begging in the Bradford streets. He wore a full-length winter overcoat and had a soft hat wrapped around his head, and he would play his clarinet for the good people of the town. Blind Jimmy apparently had his favourite spots for his performances where he could be seen at the appointed times, such was his regime. He was often seen on the steps of the old Zoar Chapel on Allerton Road, and at the entrance to the Kirkgate market.

Another open-air character in the city was the bookseller Tommy Ramsden.He had his stall in Kirkgate market, and William Scruton recalled it, when he was writing in 1890, as being there around 1865. Scruton wrote that people stopped to listen to him, to enjoy his dry humour, rather than to buy his books. His background was in the trade of auctioneer, and that explains his 'gift of the gab' but whatever charms he had, the business did not do well, and his slid into poverty. Fortunately, in that age well before the Welfare State, there were charities, and he was helped, notably by the Bradford Tradesmen's Benevolent Society, but as Scruton remarks, he died soon after he was awarded an annuity by that philanthropic body.

'Genuine' Thompson of York

There are some eccentrics and street personalities who are forgotten for some time and are then rediscovered, thanks to social historians and enthusiasts for the past. Such a one – a drunkard and public nuisance – was Robert Thompson, who was a regular in the local police courts in the early 1870s. He became known as 'Genuine' and when he reached his forty-third conviction there was a challenge in process – would he make it to fifty appearances before the 'Beak?'

He was regarded, with a strange affection, as some kind of popular champion, and was given a belt to wear. His little petty offences kept on earning him short stays behind bars, but there was a tolerance given him, and he was certain to steal again, taking very small sums, after release. By December that year he reached his forty-ninth offence which was breaking a window. Was Genuine destined to reach the half-century?

Sure enough, the local newspaper, the *Gazette*, reported on the landmark transgression, noting that 'This incorrigible offender was charged with doing damage at the Coach and Horses and he was sentenced to two months of hard labour. But the offences continued, and clearly, he was becoming an embarrassment. When out in the open air again, as historian A.J. Peacock has researched, Genuine dropped a few pegs into the realm of disgusting and shameful. The paper sums up his offence, as quoted in Peacock's essay on the man: 'That notorious fellow, Robert Henry Thompson, labourer, who had appeared before the bench fifty-three times previously, was charged with indecently exposing his person in the Shambles... Fined 10s and costs, and in default of fourteen days imprisonment.'

His fate was far from happy however, as he was to become a resident of a workhouse and defined as a lunatic. Following that, after other drunken offences, he was detained as a more dangerous lunatic, in an asylum. The press summed up the situation: 'The city has at last been purged of a pest.' Nevertheless, it is clear from the records of his activities that he stands for that type of lovable rogue that a community tends to regard with a certain degree of affection, although it is well known that the man crossed the line when it came to the law.

Mr Robertson's Peculiar Boat

Over three centuries ago, in a cold January in Leeds, a Mr Robertson entertained the public with a peculiar exhibition. The magistrates and a large crowd of over 500 people of the city gathered to watch the man swim with the use of a leather boat. One report of this impressive display by Robertson, a Scot, noted the key feature of the boat : 'the boat... before he inflated it with a pair of bellows, was so small and pliable, as to be folded up into a handkerchief, if not put into the pocket.'

The man could have been employed in one of the variety shows or feasts which toured the county, as he was a string swimmer, and was able to steer the tiny craft as he swam. But the crowd were intrigued and mystified more by the incredible folding vessel than by the swimming in the River Aire. Robertson was surely centuries before the modern equivalent, a master of the Japanese arts of miniatures and the maximization of limited space

The Davenport Brothers

'A bad turn' might best describe these unfortunate entertainers, who in 1865, when ordinary folk expected their money's worth after hard-earned cash was spent in the theatre, were in dire straits in Leeds. They managed to give their performance to a small audience at the music-hall but trouble was brewing all the way through. People knew that they had failed to turn up in Hull just before this and also at Huddersfield.

The Davenports' act was a séance, and that was always a risky business. Part of their act involved them being tied up and reef knots were used. In Leeds, they objected to those knots being used and there was dissatisfaction expressed loudly. Let the newspaper of the time tell the of main event: 'They alleged that the two gentlemen who were tying them were pulling the knots too tight and were injuring them; a scene of great excitement ensued and the two brothers hastily left the hall, and neither the inducement of their friend nor that of any other person was powerful enough to bring them back.'

The men who had trussed them mightily were Adjutant Longbolton of the Leeds Engineer Rifle Corps and Sergeant McArthur of the Royal Engineers. There was even a surgeon there to be referee. But none of these men could prevent the riot that followed the brothers' escape. Their cabinet and all their equipment was smashed to pieces by the disgruntled crowd. After the police had been called there was a loud demonstration and a local 'speculator' – the man who had booked the brothers, was forced to arrange for the crowd to have their money returned. He apparently agreed to do so, but it was never done and he played for time. As the local reporter wrote, 'It need hardly be added that the performances arranged for Saturday were not attempted... The stretching was not very agreeable to the brothers, and it was the general impression of the audience that they wanted to do the stretching themselves, this being one of the means by which they made their performance successful.'

Foster Powell the Walking Phenomenon

In the eighteenth century walking was an accepted part of life. People walked immense distances and thought nothing of it. The poet Wordsworth walked over 20 miles in a day and then more if he had to get back home. But even this pales into insignificance when compared to the achievements of Foster Powell of Horsforth. He was born there in 1734 but moved to London to start a career in law. He worked for a certain Mr Bingley and it was while he was with this gentleman that his pedestrian feats began, because he promised him that he would walk 50 miles on the road to Bath in seven hours. In 1764 he did exactly that, doing the first 10 miles in one hour.

He did not stop at that. He decided to walk great stretches of open land in Switzerland and in France; in 1773 he walked from London to York and back again in five days and four hours – that was a walk of 400 miles. This he did to win some cash in a bet.

He then graduated to running and managed to do 2 miles in ten minutes, so we have to speculate on exactly what he could achieve had he been around now, with a coach, designer equipment and specialist diets. Then off he went to the Bath road again and this time he did a hundred miles in a solid day's non-stop walking. But London to York was his favourite so he did that again in six days that time, and again in 1792. By that time he was fifty-eight years old, so he was out to beat his own record. He made it in five days and just under sixteen hours. According to a report on this, he was welcomed on his return 'with loud huzzas of the astonished and anxious spectators.'

Foster always wanted new challenges and adapted to sprinting as well, running one mile and walking another in fifteen minutes, which he did with no problems, hardly breaking into a sweat. When he really stretched himself and took on something he just could not do, he lost the bet, but actually his friends raised money for him by subscription and he came out of it well. That was when he walked from London to Canterbury but took the wrong road and got lost.

Foster had no time for wealth really; he never earned more than £10 in one time. The secret of his success appears to have been in his frugal lifestyle and eating only light food. A Victorian journal describes him in this way:

He seems to have considered his wonderful agility as a circumstance from which he derived great glory. In person he was tall and thin, about five feet nine inches, very strong downwards, well calculated for walking, and rather of a sallow complexion, in disposition he was mild and gentle and possessed many valuable qualifications.

He was usually careful and restrained but his obsession finally killed him: he overdid things in his last York walk and pushed himself too far. He only let himself have five hours' rest in the whole return journey. He was seriously ill, with a sudden collapse, in 1793, dying on 15 April that year.

His funeral was a major event in London: 'The funeral was characteristically a walking one, from New Inn, through Fleet Street and up Ludgate Hill... The attendants were all men of respectability.' Here was one of the many great eccentrics spawned by the city of Leeds, and we have to wonder why he never walked there, from London to his home town.

Woodbine Lizzie

Many Leeds folk alive today have vivid memories of this Leeds character. She was a regular sight in the city centre in the 1950s, smoking a Woodbine cigarette, with a bag over her arm, unwashed and unkempt. Her real name was Alice Porter. Now she would undoubtedly have the phrase 'Bag Lady' applied to her. But her fame must have spread very widely because in the Second World War in the desert, an army transporter was called 'Woodbine Lizzie from Leeds.'

Members of my own family recall her, as on one occasion two Wades were looking in Lewis's shop window when they became aware of a figure standing behind them. It was Lizzie, and in per posh voice she said, 'Don't they look a right sight that lot?' Another memory, posted on a website by John Hitchen, recalls her chopping wood and Mr Hitchen says she looked like 'Old Mother Riley in the movies.'

John Morgan in his book *A Celebration of Leeds* notes that the legend about her is that she was the unwanted daughter of a lord of the realm, disowned at birth. She is fixed in Leeds mythology and street history as the woman cadging 'Woodies' as she tramped the streets.

The Blind Botanist

In 1920, John Grimshaw Wilkinson was interviewed by a *Times* reporter. Wilkinson had been talked about in the recent prestigious Royal Institution lecture by Professor Bragg, so the journalist went to see the minor celebrity. The man had been blind since he was twenty-two, and he was sixty-four when interviewed. The Leeds man was self-taught in science, particularly in botany.

He was a grocer by trade but his passion was plants and on one occasion, when taken to Temple Newsam by a friend, and he showed that just by touching a tree he could name the variety. 'If I feel a poppy leaf,' he said, 'On a hot July morning it feels cold, but if I feel a leaf of London Pride at the same time it is quite warm, although the plants may be within a yard of each other. When I touch anything I note whether it is warm or cold and then I ask myself why.' During heavy showers he became aware that trees made different sounds. He told the reporter that the oak was the noisiest in a storm as it 'reflected the echoes by its leaves.'

Wilkinson's claims were quite stunning, especially in relation to touch. Not only did he say that it was a 'delight' to shake hands with some people (and he talked about a Leeds surgeon whose handshake was nervous but who could 'handle the lancet with great skill') but then he extended this interest with a reference to prisoners in Armley, saying that if he were allowed to go to that gaol, he would shake hands with the prisoners and 'at one tell which were the habitual criminals and which were not.' He explained that criminals would not be 'well balanced in action.'

There had to be something substantial and interesting in all this, as Mr Wilkinson was given a degree of M.Sc. by the University of Leeds. This remarkable man fits in well with a long line of self-taught types around Leeds; it appears to be a place that nurtures that faculty. But whatever the reasons why Mr Wilkinson developed his extraordinary powers, the point is that he did so with a scientific curiosity and a careful method of enquiry, matching his analytical mind with the strange creativity in his insights into nature. The results were astounding at times and we have to wish that he had indeed been allowed into Armley Gaol for his innovative experiments. Who knows what kind of forensics that may have opened up.

At the time there was no-one bold enough to take him up on the offer. But one feels that he would have had the confidence to impress anyone monitoring his progress with the villains.

Dentist, Welsh Bard and Poetry Lover

Charles Forshaw is remembered by few Yorkshire people today, and those who are familiar with his writings will know him as an anthologist of Yorkshire poetry rather than as a poet. He was a dental surgeon in professional life in Bradford, but the love of poetry and local history in him led to the production of a vast amount of literature on Yorkshire and on Yorkshire writers. He was not a Yorkshireman: he was born in Bilsdon, Staffordshire, on 23 January, 1863. He studied chemistry and dentistry and became a Doctor of Dental Surgery in 1885. During his time as a dentist he received many honours, including an honorary LL.D. from Tusculum University, Tennessee, and an M. D. from Chicago National Medical University. He also wrote papers on the use of cocaine and on the microscopic structure of teeth. His early biographer, J. G. Gibson, collected all the facts about the honours conferred on Forshaw and the statistics of his literary career. Gibson says that, 'He has today (1908) written over one thousand biographies of poets and poetasters… fifty publications have issued from his pen… he has contributed verses to more than 5000 journals and newspapers…'

What Forshaw wanted to do was collect poetry and fill books with it. He edited sixteen collections of poetry of various kinds, mostly occasional poems or Yorkshire poetry. His love for the collection of a wide assortment of poems on a set theme for instance, was always with him, along with poems of place and belonging. He collected anthologies of monodies on the deaths of Queen Victoria, W E Gladstone, Sir Henry Irving and many others. In the lists of his publications there are also such collections as *One Hundred of the Best Poems of the European War, by Poets of the Empire* and *Poetical Tributes on the Loss of the R M S* Titanic.

Forshaw's writings, or collections of other people's writings, are prodigious in number; yet, for all his interests in poetry, there is one sphere in which his work will always be useful and interesting – that is his interest in Yorkshire literature. In his lecture, 'Some Yorkshire Poets' (1910) a poetry recital interspersed with a few biographical remarks, he gives some account of his work as an anthologist:

In the course of issuing my collections of Yorkshire poetry I have come across upwards of two thousand Yorkshiremen who have written poetry… I have known of the millionaire Yorkshire poet – only one instance though – and I have known of poets who have died in the workhouses and prisons – all Yorkshiremen bear in mind – four of them were appointed Poet Laureate.

Above all else, Forshaw was an antiquary, a compulsive collector, but his importance does not end there. He did produce some work of literary value, and although he published half a dozen books of his own, the

Charles Forshaw, the eccentric dentist

works of value are the prose writings. His lecture, mentioned above, is a valuable source-book for anyone interested in Victorian literature, but his best-known work is in *John Hartley: Poet and Author*, and his collections of Yorkshire poets with introductions in *Poets of Keighley, Bingley and Howarth* (1891) which includes examples from the work of John Nicholson the Airedale Poet and Patrick Brontë.

In his essay on John Hartley, the celebrated founder of the *Clock Almanac* and author of *Yorkshire Ditties*, there are fine passages of lively prose, as for instance in this account of Hartley giving a lecture in Quebec:

> *The streets became rivers and traffic was stopped. One solitary individual managed to reach the hall in some way, and our Hartley waited patiently but in vain for an audience, but no-one appeared! He was not to be deterred, however, and punctually made his appearance on the platform and went through one hour and a half's entertainment to his audience of ONE.*

This work on Hartley is short, but it gives us the character of the famous dialect writer and performer perfectly. At the end of the essay there is a subscription list applying for a Civil List pension for Hartley, which includes the names of people famous in literary history, like Joseph Wright the scholar and W. S. Baring-Gould, the author of 'Onward Christian Soldiers' and curate of Horbury. Forshaw himself subscribed of course, and the warmth of his essay on Hartley suggests that the wealthy Bradford dentist probably used all his influence to help Hartley in his old age.

Throughout his writing career, Forshaw went on producing poems and compiling anthologies with admirable energy, and it seems a little sad that today his efforts have been largely forgotten. Yet in his own day he was immensely successful, becoming a Fellow of the Royal Society of Literature and Fellow of the Royal Historical Society. He was also a founder-member of the Brontë Society and the Thoresby Society. Today we might apply the name 'dilettante' to him, but linked to that was his role of committee man – maybe even a 'mover and shaker' in his own circumscribed world of letters.

All accounts of him suggest a really full life, with even a touch of romance and fantasy; much of his spare time (when not pulling teeth or gathering poems) was spent in giving lectures, editing anthologies and journals such as *Yorkshire Notes and Queries*, but there were times when he entered an entirely different world. In the Coronation year of Edward VII for instance, Forshaw was made 'King's messenger' and chosen to deliver a message from the King to the people of St Kilda. Naturally, on his return, out came pen and paper and he produced a history of St Kilda – 'for the young princes' he said.

An even more incongruous event took place in 1904, for he was made, of all things, a Welsh Bard that year at the *Gorsedd*. He was given the bardic name of *Siarl Efrog*, which means 'Charles of York' and, as if this honour was not enough, he became Chevalier of the Order of Duty in France as well. Who else could claim the title of true Yorkshireman more than this colourful and eccentric character? It seems strange that a man with so many academic honours did not produce a major work of criticism, but his work in Bradford certainly brought him fame in his time and place. He wished to be recognised above all as a poet and he kept on writing poetry, but alas, it has little worth and is forgotten. He had a clumsiness that he seemed not to be aware of, as in:

Ye confused coronets of celebrated grace
That brightly gilt the arching dome of heaven.

In his poem 'To the Stars' and in his poem 'To the London Fog' we have the lines:

Men more like goblins, ghastly, gaunt and grim,
Enshrouded and enveloped 'mid its maze.

Few people will find satisfaction in these today, but maybe he should have tried to express himself in local dialect. It could be argued that Forshaw really came into his natural role when he edited the antiquarian and historical magazine, *Yorkshire Notes and Queries* in the years around the end of the nineteenth century, and into the Edwardian period. This was a fascinating periodical concerned with all things Yorkshire, allowing correspondents to write and ask about milestones, churches, coats of arms and famous soldiers or churchmen. In short, it was about the byways of the experience of living in Yorkshire through the centuries.

Perhaps Forshaw did not realise the importance of what he was doing for future folklorists and social historians of Bradford and related places. For instance, in one issue a discussion of the tradition of selling a wife filled a page, including an account from Bradford in 1858 when a man put his wife up for sale in a beer shop in Little Horton. That note provoked a list of other instances of that kind of event (as found most famously in Thomas Hardy's novel, *The Mayor of Casterbridge*) with stories from Hull and elsewhere. The journal is an absorbing read and succeeds in the way that mixtures of odd and surprising information still do today. Forshaw had found his metier in that work, and it was very successful around the county.

No doubt Charles Forshaw will be remembered as the author of source-books for writers on Yorkshire history, and the members of the Yorkshire Dialect and Folklore societies will meet his name in their researches. His writings give us not only an opening into Victorian Bradford, but in a wider sense, they shine a light into the more obscure corners of the Victorian cast of mind. Of course, we have to wonder just how much time he had left to pursue his profession of dentist. One feels that his clients, nervous in the chair, would have had Forshaw renditions of Yorkshire poems to calm them down before the drill came into action.

Big Thanks to Eve Dawnay

In April 2016, *The Times* reported on a remarkable Yorkshire story of a place that had remained the same though all the world around it gathered pace and gave in to modernity. The village in question is West Heslerton in North Yorkshire, and the reason why the place is now a wonderful piece of 'frozen time' in which history may be seen and touched, is one Eve Dawnay.

The writer, Katie Gibbons, explained: 'Eve Dawnay, a skilled craftswoman who read French at Oxford University in the 1940s worked in Paris and London before returning to Yorkshire in 1964 when she inherited the estate in her father's will.' The result was that clearly she had a profound love for the community and its material being. The whole estate has been left to go it alone, without interference, for over fifty years; the business there generates a fair amount of profit and could be described as idyllic.

There are some odd aspects, such as the fact that the West Heslerton Hall has been unoccupied for decades, but as Tom Watson, the director of Cundalls, told *The Times*, everything has remained stable and intact because of Eve Darnay's benevolence. Tom said, 'She was very kind and the property rents have always been very low... The estate has been very much untouched... and is now a blank canvas...'

It is to be hoped that the canvas will remain blank. There are so few such locations left to us. Where they do exist, as at Navenby in Lincolnshire, where Mrs Hilda Smith's cottage offers a similar time-stopped appeal, the result is often that museum status is established. One would hope that West Heslerton carries on as a happy, unchanged community.

A Crisis and a Death Wish for the Topper

This is the story of a man who knew all about taking lives – others' lives. But he found himself, at the end of his career on a railway platform, contemplating taking his own life.

In March 1884, James Berry of Heckmondwike, wrote a letter to the prison authorities. He was a former police officer, so his letter related to his past experience, because he was applying to be an executioner. He wrote:

> *I most respectfully apply to you, to ask if you will permit me to conduct the execution of the two convicts now lying under sentence of death at Edinburgh. I was very intimate with the late Mr. Marwood.... I now have one rope which I bought from him at Horncastle and have had two made from it. I have also two pinioning straps...*

The Marwood he refers to was a Lincolnshire man who had perfected the more humane method of official hanging that made use of the long drop. In other words, he made it possible to kill by quick asphyxiation rather than by the brutal strangulation previously used. He had calculated a drop in accordance with the victim's weight. Berry was keen to step into Marwood's shoes and had learned from the master.

Since Saxon times, people had been hanged as a method of judicial death in this country. In early times it was manorial and regional, and into the early nineteenth century there were still local hangmen employed, as at York. But there was a need for a general public executioner as the Victorian period wore on and public executions ended (in 1868). As hangings began to take place inside the prisons with a medley of professional men present, the hangman was expected to be rather more competent than some of his Georgian antecedents. One York hangman called Curry was notorious for taking a drink for some Dutch courage on the day he had to hang someone on the Knavesmire, and he tended to bungle things, so that at times his clients were dangling on the rope, kicking and choking for several minutes. James Berry was always an eccentric character: restless, he moved from job to job, but in hanging he found his true vocation. As with many other men in his profession, the reasons for doing that unpleasant work were partly financial and partly related to a notion of 'national moral service.' Undoubtedly it was an occupation that provided a very lucrative second income for a working man; it was always a part-time affair, right up to the end of hanging in 1964. In Berry's case, the attractions were more income for his family, some travel, and a sense that he was ridding the world of villains.

The trade was becoming almost a job with a mystique attached by 1884 when Berry wrote his application; within a few years there was to be a reorganisation of the training of hangmen, but in Berry's career, most of the time he was quite proficient, with just a few blunders to his name. He was born in February, 1852, his father Daniel being a wool-stapler. His family were Methodists and clearly would have had a problem applying restraint and morality to young, wild James. He was always in scrapes and very nearly died when struck by a horse; he also ran away to try to have a life on the ocean waves but only reached Goole. But he did have some schooling, despite the fact that he was easily led by various tearaways around him.

As a young adult, he was attracted to the police constabulary and served in Bradford after marrying at Richmond Terrace Chapel, Horton. He did well in the force, but always tended to bear grudges and cause dissension. After a spell in Nottingham and other abortive attempts to change career, he settled on coal merchandising, and then the opportunity came along to earn some good money in the hanging trade. By 1861 there were only four capital offences left on the statute book: high treason, murder, piracy and arson in royal dockyards, but there was plenty of business for Berry. His application went to the Sheriffs of London and Middlesex in 1883 and he was called to interview at the Old Bailey. He was just beaten to the job by another man, Bartholomew Binns; in the grand tradition of drunks at the scaffold, Binns made some severe mistakes, such as his disgusting bungle of a hanging in Liverpool in 1883. Binns was later fined and disciplined, and finally sacked after another drunken excursion to Liverpool.

Berry was thus next in line and had powerful references in place; he was in office and set to do his first hanging in Glasgow, where he was to officiate at a double hanging of two poachers. He was to be on the Home Office list of executioners for seven years, from 1884 to 1891 and in that time he executed 131 people. Five of these clients were women, and the most harrowing of the latter was the hanging of Mary Lefley in Lincoln prison in May, 1884. She was only the third person he hanged, and the whole affair was most alarming and upsetting for all concerned. Mary constantly protested her innocence of killing her husband and the officials at the prison were also convinced of her innocence. Berry was the first hangman to write any memoirs and he gives a shocking account of the occasion there:

> *Imagine my feelings when I went to the condemned cell to prepare her for her doom. I know that my hands trembled as the turnkey held open the door, and my tongue clove to the roof of my mouth as I essayed speech.*
>
> *Mary Lefley was in bed. She had been too ill to get up that morning and we had to shake her into consciousness. She looked round with dazed eyes as we told her to arise.*

Mary Lefley screamed and wailed all the way to the scaffold, crying, 'God knows I am innocent' She yelled that if they hanged her they would be committing murder.

James Berry,
the hangman who
planned suicide

Berry said that nine years after her death, a farmer confessed to the crime on his deathbed. Berry must have lost the ability to enjoy a peaceful night's sleep after that; it had been a horrible experience, hanging a women screaming out her innocence as the bell tolled for her death and crowd outside hushed for a few seconds.

Berry's most celebrated failure was in the case of John Lee at Exeter gaol. This happened in February 1885. Lee was just nineteen and was convicted for the murder of his female employee; on the first attempt to hang him, the lever was pulled but there was no movement on the trapdoor. The young man had to be returned to the death cell until adjustments were made. Back he came again, and that time the same thing happened again. Lee was taken away again. One final attempt was made, and still the trap would not open. The whole affair was aborted until a decision was made higher up the chain of authority. He was, understandably, spared any other execution session and was reprieved. It was learned later that a hinge had failed to work. The chaplain expressed the situation succinctly: 'For the third time I had concluded the service; for the third time the prisoner had felt the agonies of death; for the third time the responsible officers had failed to out him to death.' Lee was released in December, 1907, married a nurse, but the relationship did not work out. We know that he died in America, forgotten. But since then historians have written extensively about the case. Poor Berry simply wrote, 'The noise of the bolts could plainly be heard but the doors did not fall.'

Berry had a most horrendous experience in the attempted hanging of Robert Goodale at Norwich in 1885. The murderer was a very large man – fifteen stones – and the drop calculation was wrong. Goodale was decapitated. The terrible business made Berry resign from his post. He wrote:

> *The warder who had been assisting me had been standing too near the trap door, and the weight of the victim had pulled him over. He was clutching the sides of the opening, and it was only by the mercy of providence that he did not crash down to the foot of the well. It was the first accident of the kind that I had ever had, and I was unable to go to his assistance. Hand and brain refused to move. I stood there as if rooted to the spot...*

Berry carried out his last execution in Winchester in August, 1891, hanging Edward Fawcett. But his own last years were a sad contrast; he was at one point suicidal (a fate common to many hangmen) and by an amazing intervention of fate, he was saved.

Surely one of the most dramatic and compelling stories of this complex man's life is the account of his reclamation, spiritually, after walking out of his home one day with the intention of taking his own life. He wrote in his memoirs, 'I could not have thought it possible that mortal man could become so low and depraved... My burning conscience accused me of having wronged my family – my innocent, good and virtuous wife, and my sorely suffering children – with my carryings on in sin and wickedness. There was nothing else for it – I must put an end to my life.'

What happened was that, as he sat on a railway platform, intending to throw himself from the window of a train in a tunnel between Leeds and Bradford, he began to pray for help and guidance, and a man came onto the platform who was in fact an evangelist. He sat with Berry and somehow a shared and very public prayer, with a gathering crowd, led to his being taken in for help by a man who ran a mission hall. In short, Berry found his spiritual redemption on that railway platform; his life was saved and he became a changed man.

He published one more book after his autobiography: a short one called *Mr J Berry's Thoughts Above the Gallows,* published in 1905. This was a tract against hanging and a clear assertion of a path to salvation, willed out of his past life, both public and private. There is a quiet desperation running through everything he wrote, but this final work maintains that thread of eccentricity that was always in him, with a discussion of one of his latest fads, phrenology. He was then an evangelist, but the paraphernalia of his main occupation lingered on through time, a batch of his possessions being exhibited in a Nottingham junk shop in 1948, and in the 1950s, Berry's granddaughter still had some relics of Berry's to pass on.

He died on 21 October, 1913.

CHAPTER FOUR

Total Failures and Horrendous Disasters

EVERYONE MAKES MISTAKES, we are always told that. To be human is to get things wrong, at least sometimes. There seems to be no evidence that Tykes make more mistakes than the average Britisher, but of course in the Yorkshire chronicles there are terrible errors, often with grave consequences, and one such event, involving what West Riding folk call 'spice' – or sweets – was a major disaster, and this opens my next section of tales. But there is no escaping the fact that getting it wrong, doing a blooper, or dropping a clanger, can be very entertaining. After all, one of the consistent best-sellers in the bookshops for many years now has been Stephen Pile's *Book of Heroic Failures*.

The Gig at Hull Goes Wrong

One of the most colourful literary characters of the Victorian years was one of Dickens's protégés George Augustus Sala, a man with an Italian family history who became one of the movers and shakers of the world of journalism and of popular illustration, and perhaps most famously, as one of the *Daily Telegraph's* most illustrious foreign correspondents. But he was not always rich and famous. He had known great poverty and deprivation, and in his early years he was a risk-taker and entrepreneur. He had many business ventures which failed, and one of them was launched in Hull.

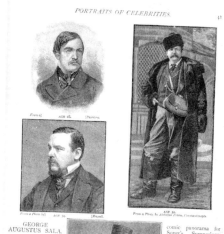

George Augustus Sala,
as profiled in The Strand

At the Assembly Rooms in 1851, not long before the Great Exhibition, George and his aeronaut friend, the charismatic but doomed Lieutenant Gale, promised the Hull public a lecture and a display on this travel of the future – the hot-air balloon. At the time, people were still full of the magnificent but sad tale of Sir John Franklin and his crew who had failed in their attempt to sail the North West Passage and were lost. All kinds of schemes were suggested to try to find those nautical heroes, and Gale's contribution was to take a balloon on board a steam-ship, and launch surveys from the deck, to look for the lost ships, HMS *Erebus* and HMS *Terror*.

Gale and Sala expected a good turn-out, but unfortunately, the people of that great maritime city were not keen on the idea. As George wrote in his memoirs, 'The night came, and I was money-taker at the Assembly Rooms. Anxiously did I listen for the sound of footsteps ascending the stairs; but I am afraid, in the whole body of the hall and gallery all round, our audience did not muster more than six and twenty, including half a dozen fisher-lads, who paid half-price and the inevitable old lady with the crush-bonnett...'

It must have been a great disappointment for the two young men, fired with enthusiasm. Sala had written the text of the lecture, and Gale had a few exhibits to impress the locals. But it was not only a poor audience, but an aggressive one. Sala explained:

> *The worst of it was, that sitting in my money-taker's box, with nothing to do, I could hear the sonorous voice of Lieutenant Gale echoing through the almost empty hall, and interrupted at no infrequent intervals by cries of 'Yah!' 'Shut up!' 'Put your head in a bag!' and so forth. Soon I was to hear another voice, tuned to tones quite as hostile. It was the voice of the local confectioner. 'Where's the five-and-twenty-bob?'*

George had given a confectioner the pitch and charged him twenty-five shillings. All he could do was sit tight in the box until the man was bored and went home.

As for poor Lieutenant Gale, he was fated to die in his ballooning exploits. He accepted an offer to display his talents in the art in France, and he was to perish. George noted that his friend '... ascended and came to grief; he fell out of the car, and his dead body was discovered a few days afterwards, half-devoured by dogs, in a wood.'

The Battle of Flamborough Head

We would have to look long and hard across the great span of history to find an adventurer with as much courage and derring-do as John Paul Jones, the Scot from Kirkbean who took on the British Navy and became an American hero. He was born in 1747 and while still under thirty he was first mate on a slaving ship. But his momentous place in history came off Flamborough Head in 1779.

When the War of American Independence began he was in the service of the colonies, and he was on board their first flagship, the *Alfred*. But he then took command of the *Bonhomme Richard* and he made a declaration that sums up his dauntless spirit. He said, 'I wish to have no connection with any ship that does not sail fast for I intend to go in harm's way.' He was definitely in harm's way when he sailed along the East Coast by Flamborough, because the British Navy faced him, and the ship which faced him in close combat was the *Serapis*. He knew that his ships were going to be beaten, but he confronted the *Serapis* and refused to give in. The fight became known as the Battle of Flamborough Head. The place is known mainly today for its proximity to the wonderful bird sanctuary at Bempton, but in 1779 it was at sea off that magnificent line of cliff that Jones, on being told that surrender was his best option, said, 'I'll sink, but I'll be damned if I will strike.'

Captain Pearson was in charge of the British vessel and he must have been very confident of success, but the Americans were determined to relish the scrap. A seaman somehow managed to hurl a grenade down the hatch of the *Serapis* and of course there were serious consequences, including the death of around twenty British tars. It was a stalemate really, because there were heavy casualties on both sides: Jones had 150 dead and wounded, and Pearson had 130 dead out of his full complement of 244. Although Pearson surrendered, it is clear that both forces were severely maimed in the encounter. The arithmetic of death always seems unacceptably bland, as real people turn into statistics.

This was not the end of Jones' roistering career though. He went on to become appointed United States Consul to Algiers, but died before he could take up the duties. But before that, surprisingly, he was a considerable presence in the navy of Catherine the Great, Empress of Russia. He died in 1792. John Paul Jones might be an American icon, known to every schoolboy in the States, but he won his gallant reputation off the Yorkshire coast in that desperate confrontation.

The Cannon King

In the heady days of the Victorian music hall, when acts appeared in the provincial theatres ready to entertain by the most extreme means, from fire-eating and sword-swallowing to walking the high wire, along came a man who was destined to catch the limelight wherever he went – mainly because his act was surely the most outrageous and foolhardy one ever recorded on the boards. It would certainly never have been booked for the BBC's *Good Old Days* from the Leeds City Varieties. This act was the brainchild of Herr Holtum, known to the theatrical profession and to the audience as Herr Holtum, The Cannon King.

In 1885 he appeared at the Circus, in Percy Street, Newcastle, Australia, and there he offered a spectacular show, *The War in the Sudan*, in which, as the local paper reported, we have this:

> *The Arabs appear first, and addressed by one of the sheiks, are urged to drive from their native soil the British invaders. After their exit, General Graham and the British soldiers appear... The scene at this point afforded an opportunity for the herculean feats of Herr Holtum (who enacts the part of Sergeant Braveheart).*
>
> *With heavy cannon balls... the feat assigned to Herr Holtum last night was what he accustomed to do nightly: everything prepared and the gun ready, Herr Holtum himself gave the order to fire and the ball was discharged. It was seen to pass uncomfortably close to his head, and it landed with a dull thud.... But it was noticed that Herr Holtum ran speedily and somewhat dazed from the spot...*

Yes, that is true: his act was that he caught cannon balls. Clearly his own life was at risk, but five years before this, he had found himself in court at the West Riding sessions charged with the unlawful wounding of a local man, Elijah Fenton.

Herr Holtum had offered the massive sum of £50 (around £600 in 2016) to anyone who could catch a 9-pound cannon ball on stage. Mr Fenton and others accepted the challenge, being of true Yorkshire grit and game for a lark. This happened at the Princess Concert Hall in Leeds, and the consequence of the act of bravado was that Fenton was battered by the ball and knocked down. Amazingly, it struck his head and he survived. But of course he was rushed to hospital. One newspaper report noted, 'He was conveyed to the Infirmary, where it was found that his skull was fractured, and that he had received injuries to his nose. He is still under medical care.'

Herr Holtum was Danish, being born in Hadersley in 1866. We may glean something of his crazed performance and his fortitude when we consider his words to the audience after a near-death experience: 'Tonight I have got a wound, and I shall be all right again, I hope, for tomorrow night... it would not have happened if I had had sufficient practice for this piece, but I have only been practising three days with the guns. It is, however, only a skin wound.'

We have no record of whether or not Mr Fenton survived, but certainly, The Cannon King was remembered in Leeds for a long time.

Mass Deaths after James gets it Wrong

In November, 1858 young James Archer was sent by his boss to bring some mixture used in the confection of sweet lozenges. The businessman who sent the boy, one Mr Neale of Shipley, had been earlier to the premises with him, and he had pointed out that one barrel in the store-room was the substance used – a mixture called 'daff' – and another, in a similar barrel, was arsenic. Clearly, this was a very important distinction to make. Daff was otherwise known as terra alba (literally, 'white earth') and was a form of plaster of Paris.

James returned later to collect some daff, and the man who kept the store, a Mr Hodgson, was too ill to assist, so he sent the lad down to collect the material himself. James could see the barrels, but he could not see any label to tell him which was arsenic. The label was actually on the base of the heavy barrel, out of sight. But he saw a barrel of a white substance, and collected twelve pounds to take back to his master.

The lozenges were made by Neale and then sold on to local retailers. A few days later, fifteen local people were dead and many more seriously ill. Many of them had bought their lozenges from the Green Market on the Saturday night, just after they were made, from trader called Hardaker. As soon as the morning after, two deaths were reported – both children: Elijah Wright (nine) and Joseph Scott (fourteen). The result was complete panic in the streets. A speedy and massive police operation was put into place. It was a rare challenge: how did you let people know they were likely to be nibbling sweets loaded with arsenic? It was a simple matter to trace the lozenges from Hardaker to Neale, whose premises were in Manor Row (Stone Street); but the Chief Constable, Mr Leveratt, and Copeland, the Superintendent, soon went to work in a desperately important communication exercise. All available officers set about walking the streets to warn everyone they met on their normal beats; men set out with bells to announce the horrible accident, and bills were posted up, informing everyone passing about the deadly sweets. Hardaker still had thirty-six pounds of the stuff, and this was recovered. Townsfolk were bringing the deadly objects in to the law as time went on, but on Sunday there were over one hundred cases reported of people suffering the ill effects.

The amazing thing is that, in the process of manufacture, no-one had suspected anything to be wrong. One James Appleton had been close to the substances as they were mixed, and he had suffered severe sickness for eight hours as he worked with gum, sugar and peppermint, with the arsenic powder churning and spraying around him. Still no-one thought to think about this unusual outcome in the process. There ought to have been some suspicion when Hardaker brought some of the sweets to Neale to point out that they were not the usual colour. He was given them at a discount for that reason, and the sales went forward. On sale, they sold at two ounces for three pence and the business was brisk.

The case came to court and Neale faced a charge of manslaughter through negligence. At the Court House, Bradford, Inspector Burnieston reported on going to investigate the room where the two barrels had been kept. The prosecution were going to have to prove gross negligence if there was to be a conviction. This means that there would have to be behaviour of a kind 'substantially worse than that of the average reasonable man.' An accused would have to be shown to have appreciated a certain risk he was taking in the conduct of his behaviour, rather than a kind of understandable thoughtlessness or error. The inspector realised that, tracing the actions of the young assistant, he could not see a label, and the weight of the barrel was 2 cwt, too heavy to lift. So, the young man would not have seen the label. The crucially important detail then was that arsenic was usually coloured, mixed with a dye, rather than left its normal white colour. All was clear then. James had been looking for a white substance and he had found it. His knowledge did not extend to an acquaintance with arsenic and its treatments or storage. Two medical men at the trial found very large quantities of arsenic in the lozenges. Each lozenge had about nine and a half grains of arsenic in it; this was more than enough to kill a person. But

A satirical drawing on the easy purchase of arsenic Punch

it must be said that there were other troublesome factors in this case, such as the finding of chromate of lead in the sweets under examination. There had been attempts to improve and regulate the manufacture of such sweets in Glasgow not long before this, and in that city there was, in 1858, a union formed to prevent the use of daff in the making of the lozenges.

The Arsenic Act of 1851 had not made it clear who actually were to be called 'pharmacists', to avoid the easy access to the poison by ordinary people, so anyone known as a druggist (like Neale) could store and sell it.

The result of all this was a shocking death toll. As the trail went on at the Borough Court, inquests took place also, and in the end there were twenty deaths and more than two hundred illnesses caused by this awful accidental negligence – and so it was – not *gross* negligence. At the Assizes, before Mr Baron Watson, it was decided that there was no need for a jury; as everything said had shown that Neale had reminded his assistant about the arsenic. He had also shown the young man where the two barrels were placed. It was an unfortunate series of circumstances that led to many tragic deaths. The boy's testimony revealed an ignorance of all technical matters concerned. Neale would have to be acquitted of gross negligence, and in fact Baron Watson stated that he could see nothing that suggested negligence of any kind. As was confirmed in the summing up, Neale had 'warned his young man that the cask contained arsenic.' In the end it was simply that all would have been well if Hodgson had stirred from his bed and supervised the collection of the substance down in his store-room. But that is with hindsight, and does nothing to alleviate the awful suffering caused by this.

If it hadn't been for the quick thinking and common sense of officers Leveratt and Copeland, the death toll could have been treble what it was. As for the offending lozenges: the editor of a magazine several years later reported that he had some in his possession as dark mementos of one of Bradford's most horrendous poisoning cases.

Engulfed

Inside a bend of land, west of Kilnsea on the East Yorkshire coast, the lost villages of Holderness lie beneath the waves. Under those wide flats, as the Spurn Railway was being built, were the settlements of Orwithfleet, Synthorpe, Ravenser and Ravenser Odd. Of these places, Ravenser Odd has attracted most historical interest. This trading town, was a major seaport before the growth of Hull. The Humber floods did not hit the place until the mid-fourteenth century; before then, it was an important port and had its own M.P. An inquisition of Edward III contains this information in a writ to the servants responsible for tax-gathering in his domain:

> *Whereas recently we have learned that the town has been daily diminished by frequent inundations of the water of the sea surrounding the said town, and the soil there of great quantity has been carried away, and that 145 buildings which belong to Cecily de Selby... and forty-two places not built upon... which said buildings and places constituted two parts and more of the aforesaid town, have been taken by the sea by such inundations and the flux of the said waters, from the eighth year of King Edward... and the people have withdrawn from that town by reason of such waste and impoverishment that they are not able in any way to support or pay the tenths and tolls...*

The King was tolerant. He asked for only one hundred shillings. But as is easily inferred from this, Ravenser Odd was a large-scale community. In fact, despite the fact that in the Domesday Book of 1086 there were no Holderness boroughs, by c. 1250 there were three – Hedon and Skipsea along with Ravenser Odd. These places were founded by the family of Aumale, who had been given burgage charters by the English kings. This

Map of the Humber Estuary

meant that the landowners of the locality held land by paying an annual rent to the sovereign; this was not fully abolished until 1925.

Ravenser Odd is one of many ports recorded in this area in early times. One of the most vague and elusive is 'Cornu Vallis' which was a Saxon port referred to by Ceolfrid's scribe back in the seventh century. All we know of it today, as Richard Muir has put it, is that 'it is lost'. Ravenser itself figures prominently in the story of 1066 however; it was from here (then called Hrafnseri in Old English) that Harald Hardrada sailed home after being defeated just outside York at Stamford Bridge in that year, before Harold sped down south to his doom at Hastings.

Ravenser Odd has gone, but along the Holderness coast, the line of villages on the edge of the land continue to provide stories of threatened dissolution and ruin. One of the most striking declines has been the story of Skipsea. Here was a notable castle, built by Drogo de la Beuvriere, and although its demolition was ordered in 1221, the place was always

101

important because of the notion of castle guard. This phrase defined the military holding, created after the 1066 conquest, in the framework of Norman power across the land. This meant that the holder of the castle guard tenure acted for the king. In the 1200s, knights in Holderness gave knight service and castle guard to their sovereign. In the early medieval centuries, records give mention to the castle guard at Skipsea.

Skipsea was once the main residence of the Lord of Holderness; forty years ago, a local writer noted that the place was then 'little more than an uneasy summer retreat of chalets and bungalows perched precariously above the beach.' Today, as a newspaper report stated in 2011, the situation there is that at least twenty homes will be in the sea within the next century. Between Flamborough and Spurn – 45 miles – it has been estimated that 200 homes are under threat. The University of Hull has gathered a collection of photos giving evidence of the sea's devouring of coastal roads, and academics there have been busy estimating the rate of land-loss over the next decades.

Nearby Hornsea is full of historical interest, and owes its popularity as a resort chiefly to a Hull entrepreneur called Joseph Wade. His cash from a timber company helped to finance the building of a railway from Hull to Hornsea, opened in 1864. But Hornsea, now perhaps most famous for its pottery, goes back a very long way as a settlement. In the late fourteenth century it was the fifth largest place in the East Riding of Yorkshire.

Erosion is a constant threat, and in fact, a related settlement, Hornsea Beck, has been completed lost and is on the list of the ghostly former villages of Holderness; it was first mentioned in 1228, and not long after that there was a weekly market, part of a charter gained by St Mary's Abbey. Poll Tax records show a population of 264 people in 1377 – a slightly larger number than that of Hornsea itself. It was in the fifteenth century that erosion began to be a problem. It has been calculated that between 1546 and 1609, 38 properties were lost to the waves. One of the ways in which we know of a footnote in the historical record is through legal documents, and sure enough, it is the court rolls which in this case indicate that Hornsea Beck was close to its final stage of decline in the mid-eighteenth century.

In 2011, the north country journalist and writer Martin Wainwright wrote a feature for the *Guardian* on the Holderness lost villages, and he listed 29 lost villages, which had first been listed by Thomas Sheppard, writing in 1912. The erosion problems are at a desperate stage, yet as Wainwright notes, there is just one consolation – at least for Lincolnshire people – that '... much of the debris from the coast is washed round Spurn Point and into the Humber, reinforcing the delicate-looking peninsula and creating new land from the estuary in the area of Sunk Island.'

If we have to pinpoint one place which contains all the woes and trials of being potentially a village lost in the sea, we go to Aldborough, just 6 miles south of Hornsea. Already, three hotels have fallen into the sea – the Spa, the Talbot and the Royal. Old Aldborough has already gone. Today, the seaside road has been eaten away and is blocked off at the cliff edge. The British Geological Survey is giving the place a great deal of attention.

The Survey records that 'The cliffs are receding and the cliff profile is stepped due to the contrasting erosion resistances of the tills... in same cases middle sections of the cliff are subject to considerable erosion by wave action.' The caravan site has received some attention also; the Survey authors conclude that a study of maps shows that 'Using data going back to 1786, up to two million square metres a year were removed from the cliff...' There have also been, naturally, severe landslides.

Looking at the historical records for Aldborough, the efforts in the Victorian years to develop the place as a seaside holiday location were adventurous and optimistic, but met with little success. In 1832 there was a beer house near the sea. Robert Raikes began to build a hotel at that time, and that became the Talbot; sea-bathing began and from 1846 the Spa Inn was established; there were attempts to lift the place into the category of spa town. There was an omnibus service from Hull in the 1840s, and three lodging houses are recorded then. But its competitor, Hornsea, won the race for the title of a 'seaside place for Hull.'

Dangerous Victorian Leeds

The new industrial conurbations in the West Riding were dangerous places. Not only was there pollution in the foul air and the peril of lethal machines at places of work: there were also the streets themselves, badly lit, often packed with detritus, and infested with both rats and thieves. If we add to the mix the widespread availability of strong drink, with beer-shops and inns at every corner, then the frequency of horrendous accidents and disasters is not surprising. Some stories from Leeds in the nineteenth century will illustrate some of these dangers. First, this from 1885.

On a Monday afternoon in this year about 150 people were skating on a huge pond at Gledhow on a large estate owned by a man called Cooper. The pool was 500 yards by 100 yards in dimensions and the owner of the place was quite happy for all and sundry to come and use it. After large numbers had used it on this fateful day, Mary Jane Balmer, just sixteen years old, came to join in the fun, some young medical students being with her.

There was an assistant of her father (a surgeon) with her to keep an eye on things, but some fun started when a chair, in the possession of the medical students, was pushed out onto the ice. A student called George Broughton pushed Mary Jane's sister, and then Jane herself, around on this chair. But when they were around 12 yards from the edge, the ice broke and the water where they were was about 14 feet deep. Mary Jane and a man of twenty-eight, Lyndon Smith, went down under the water.

Several people present tried hard to save them; the man Broughton shoved Mary Jane into the danger area, but then to his credit he went in after her. The newspaper report of the time said,

> *His head could be seen above the water, but he was lost because the ice kept breaking whenever he attempted to get out. Mr G Broughton fell into the water at the same time as Miss Balmer but his brother retrieved him with a stick... all the twenty or so persons on the ice at the time disappeared...*

Broughton tried hard to help anyone he could. At one point a hand came up through the broken ice and he did his best to help, but it was all in vain.

But of course no-one had considered the possibility of an accident. It was a carefree atmosphere. There were no ropes or long pieces of wood present for such an event. But after some time, two men called Rhodes and Naylor stripped and went in, seeing the increasingly desperate situation. The reporter who spoke to one of them later noted that the man thought during the ordeal that he had a body in his grasp but it turned out to be a coat. The place where the bodies had gone down was discussed and considered to be the most dangerous part of the pond.

It was ninety minutes after the two people went down that the bodies were finally recovered; the coroner said at the inquest that there had been 'no precipitancy or rashness on the part of Mr Broughton' and the poor man had done all he could to save young Mary Jane. There was strong advice about ropes and poles being placed at the ready for the next time skating might happen at Cooper's pool.

Leeds was full of talk about the story for some time. A letter was written to *The Times* two days after the tragedy, in which a person signed as 'Jacques' wrote: 'I am led to suggest the following simple and cheap precaution for all semi-public skating places.' His solution was a plank.

That may not have been revolutionary but he was sure of the benefits: 'Let a plank of deal, 11 inches wide and 17 or 18 feet long, be placed at or near the pond… In the event of a break in the ice the plank is shoved across the fracture and affords safe support to those succouring and those immersed.'

All very wise, but too late to help poor Mary Jane and Lyndon Smith.

In 1838 some almshouses were constructed on Holbeck Moor. They were not made because some local philanthropist had money to spare. They were done as a result of extreme need following a massive disaster.

The 1830s were a dark period in the history of the working class. Not only was there a problem with the price of food – it was very high – but there were Chartist actions and a spate of crimes in rural areas. On top of all that, in Holbeck, there was a massive explosion in Blackburn's Yard, as a fireworks maker's factory blew up. The power of the blast was so intense that windows and doors all across Leeds shook and shivered; it must have seemed to some folk that the end of the world was nigh. But in fact the tragedy happened because Susannah Dockray blew out a candle. She did so, thoughtlessly, in the room where the gunpowder was stored. Before any really noisy blast disrupted anyone, the poor girl ran out into the yard, her frock on fire, to a background of crackling noises.

Then other young women joined in the panic and ran out with Susannah, but we have to wonder at a Mrs Wood, because she scrambled back into the danger zone, perhaps hoping to stop things escalating to the point at which the whole place would be blown to hell. But she was too late. The factory was splattered into fragments in the Holbeck air. Of course, Mrs Wood was killed, along with her child. Other places nearby suffered extreme damage as well. Members of families around the factory were fortunate that they were not in vulnerable positions when the explosion happened: James Walker, for instance, was buried under a pile of rubble. Other people did die, however, including a man of seventy.

In 1866 in Dewsbury Road, two men died as a result of a boiler explosion at the Frogland Mungo Works. Casualties were high in addition to the deaths, as eighteen women were also maimed. The engineman was Samuel Pearson and the rag machine tenter was Benjamin Preston; they took quite a while to die, expiring in hospital on the day after the disaster. What the coroner and the papers wanted to know was whether there was any suspicion that the boiler was faulty in any way.

The men had died in agony. Pearson had serious burns on his face and body and Pearson had a compound fracture of his left thigh bone. What remained when their manner of death was described and surgeons asked about actions taken, was to start an enquiry about the boiler's condition, so the court initiated that process, two engineers being employed to test the place and look at the evidence. The court was adjourned until that was done and results given. Some of the men who reported later were of very good professional standing, such as Mr Manning of the Institute of Mechanical Engineers. The worst fears were to be confirmed.

The Yorkshire Post explained the nature of the problem which had caused the explosion: 'The fixed load upon the small valve was not excessive, supposing the boiler to have been in good condition. He (Mr Manning) had no hesitation in saying that the explosion was caused by the weakening of the boiler by the secret extensive corrosion.' What should have been done, it was commented, was that there should have been a periodic inspection, but these matters were not so strictly enforced then. Even more paradoxical by today's standards, the matters related to safe maintenance of such fixtures and plant was sidelined, as a story emerged about one Joshua Goodall lighting his pipe.

The verdict was accidental death. Nothing came from statements given by tradesmen about noted leaks and malfunctions of the boiler, which was, it was claimed, just five years old. The Health and Safety Executive of today would be shivering with indignation should they read this.

The Victorian period was also the time when poisons were not really handled and regulated with much care and attention. Often children and servants would collect medicines and be open to getting things wrong. In the Bradford case described earlier, in which poison accidentally was mixed into a recipe for making boiled sweets, the deaths were in double figures. Sometimes the errors were down to illiteracy, and quantities were wrongly prepared. In one case in Leeds, Mr Haigh of Richmond Hill was lucky not to die as a result of a mistake.

In 1868 he took some laudanum which he thought was tincture of rhubarb. A neighbour of Mr Haigh, called Barnes, had died as a result of taking the mixture from the very same bottle that Haigh drank from. What had happened was that Barnes had a problem with diarrhoea and the tincture was to put that right. A handbook of remedies of that time states that rhubarb 'is given internally for diarrhoea' and that 'one to four drachms' should be given as a tincture for a 'debilitated state of the bowels.' Mr Barnes thought he was having exactly that, but he died. Barnes, as the doctor's report made clear, had died from diarrhoea, 'the deceased having ejected laudanum from his stomach.' The origin of the death and near-death was in the incompetence of a young assistant who had carelessly filled the bottle with laudanum instead of the rhubarb tincture.

In industrial Leeds in these perilous years of the mid-Victorian times, children were always especially vulnerable when adults were going about the daily grind. Young Jane Scatchard and her fate are a nasty example of this: she was simply walking past the Anchor of Hope Inn in Leylands when the landlord, Mr Woodson, decided to wash his barrels. Little Jane was only five years old, and she thought that this would be a good place to play, so she took hold of a barrel but then fell in – the water was scalding hot. She fell into the water head first. The girl suffered intense agony for four hours before she died of the burns. The *Leeds Mercury* reported that 'The jury, in returning a verdict of accidental death severely censured Mr

Woodson for washing his barrels in the public footpath, a thing which Mr Emsley [coroner] said was against the law, and must not be repeated.

In those years, when factories, shops and all kinds of industries were being made and set out in all kinds of haphazard ways, with no thought but for the efficiency of the production process, Leeds people were living on the edge, exposed to all kinds of noxious vapours, chemicals and noises. They would spend their working day in intense noise and breathe in effluents; they would risk being at the mercy of incompetent professionals sometimes in the health services and they would face dangers every time they were in any built-up area. Often, their medicine was as dangerous as the illnesses they had, and employers could subject them to high risk activities without proper protection. The years of the Victorian heyday of industry were certainly years of living dangerously.

Of course, families grew wiser to all this as they became involved in the world of work and were getting an education. Better levels of literacy obviously helped people to be aware of the whole range of potential dangers lurking in the workplace and indeed in the home. Public health had improved by those last decades of the century but the workplace was still packed with danger.

Many of the real 'heroes' of the city are surely unknown now, because they were the people in everyday work who fought to improve these things and to have some kind of justice and fairness in their work within perilous places. Some of these places, such as mines, would not really be regulated and controlled for some time to come in this era of Victorian prosperity – a prosperity that was often built on high risk and great danger to the individuals caught up in that huge industrial state, feeding and supplying not just England, but her vast Empire across the map that was painted red.

Then there were the effects and harrowing suffering brought about by things not at all connected to the Industrial Revolution, such as the death of Matilda Wormald, aged only twenty-eight. Matilda had been living what her father described as an 'irregular life' – that is she had left home and been on her own in various places. In early January 1880, she went to the home of Eliza Gee in Mabgate and asked Eliza for a bed for the night. Eliza, co-habiting, not married, managed to sort that out for her. But poor Matilda was so ill the next day that Eliza let her stay for most of the week.

Matilda went on, clearly very feeble and at the end of her tether and she was seen by another woman called Wormald, whose partner was rather more callous than previous men, saying, 'You will not have to stay here' followed by his actually turfing her out into the street with the words, 'We will not have you here any more.' This was at least how it was according to one witness, but Wormald denied it, saying that he told the woman he could not afford to keep her there. Matilda Wormald was found dead in a deserted house. The local paper described what happened: 'On Friday afternoon police constable Watmuff was called to the house, number 70 Mabgate at present unoccupied, where he saw a woman named Matilda Wormald, apparently in a dying state. The officer sent to Millgarth station and Mr Hollingworth, one of the police surgeons, was telegraphed for but when he arrived life was extinct. The body was removed to the mortuary ...' She had pneumonia – technically lobar pneumonia, and doctors then could do nothing about that. What most upset the jury at the coroner's court was the 'cruel treatment meted out to the dying woman.'

The Albert Medal won at Sheffield

On 18 May, 1889, John Smith, a labourer at Siemens works, part of Thomas Firth's plant, found himself tested to the extreme, and his efforts were to win him the Albert Medal. He and his mates were shifting a red-hot steel ingot from a casting pit when a man, Ben Stanley, slipped and fell fifteen feet down into the pit by the ingot. He was almost knocked unconscious by the fall, and of course, the heat soon started to consume him.

John Smith didn't stop to think: he followed his friend down, using a ladder. He was naked to the waist, and had no special protection; in fact, his haste made the ladder spin round and he slithered down, not fully in control of his movements. But such was his courage and agility that he reached Ben, lifted him up and scrambled across to the next pit in the line. From there, they could be lifted to safety.

Naturally, both men were badly burnt. John managed to survive but Ben died of his burns. One report of the time makes an important point: '...the inner pit into which John boldly dashed was the place which immediately surrounded the bottom of the great steel ingot – depth down of three feet and a width from the wall to the ingot of only two feet, three inches.'

John Smith was later given a reward of over forty pounds. The hero had lifted a man from a tiny space, not much more than a yard, with the ultra-hot ingot uncomfortably close to the men's flesh. The man was indeed a true hero, and a worthy recipient of the Albert Medal. This was the civilian equivalent of the Victoria Cross, and had been instituted by Royal Warrant on 7 March, 1866, but that was at first related only to gallantry at sea. Therefore, in April, 1867, a second class was created, extending the award to acts of bravery in any context. Consequently there were two classes: Albert Medal First Class – Sea, and the equivalent for Land.

John Smith thoroughly deserved that gold, oval badge, enamelled in dark blue with the letters V and A interlaced. Other Yorkshiremen in the later years of Victoria's reign were to win the medal, including Ambrose Clarke and Robert Drabble, of Rotherham, after their extraordinary and courageous action at a pit shaft accident at Rotherham Main in 1891.

A Trio of Yorkshire Tykes and Sir Walter Scott

One of the aspects of the life and work of Sir Walter Scott, author of the Waverley novels and major cultural and literary figure in the Romantic period, is that he experienced bankruptcy. The story of his determination to write and earn enough to keep himself solvent, and to keep his wonderful home of Abbotsford on the River Tweed is legendary. Surely never did a man work so doggedly and industriously to keep his head above water and keep out of the debtors' prison.

The beginning of his problems in this respect were in his enterprise in joining friends in a printing firm, John Ballantyne & Co. As Margaret Drabble explains, ' In 1826 James Ballantyne & Co. became involved in the bankruptcy of Constable and Co and Scott, as partner of the former, found himself liable for a debt of about £114,000. He shouldered the whole burden himself and henceforth worked heroically, shortening his own life by his strenuous efforts ...'

What is not so well know is that three businessmen from Leeds were involved in the story, led by a man called James Ogle Robinson. Robinson, with Hurst, his first partner, were agents for Constable's books, based in London, and from their office in Cheapside they began to publish topographical books as well as acting as agents. In 1968, Frank Beckwith, in the *University of Leeds Review*, set about making the 'Three Tykes' as Scott called Thomas and John Hurst, together with Robinson, better known. Beckwith found out that Thomas Hurst did not fare well, as an obituary states from 1847: ' He died in the Charterhouse, to the refuge of which he was driven by his unfortunate connexion with the house of his brother, Hurst, Robinson & Co.'

There is no doubt that Robinson was at the heart of this sad episode for Scott and others. Beckwith recalled that Joseph Robinson, born 1787, started as a librarian and bookseller in Leeds and was linked with the Leeds Library. The Leeds Library, with the influence of Robinson and his friend Alaric Watts, bought dozens of copies of the Waverley novels between 1813 and 1829, so they were doing their bit for Scott.

The problems for Scott had come when James Ballantyne raised money with the use of accommodation bills, and many of these were coming from Hurst and Robinson. An accommodation bill is a bill of exchange which entails a third party sanction of approval. Hurst and Robinson were providing these, when of course, they were in the red themselves. But their 'front' was that they were publishers of lavishly illustrated volumes, signifying a touch of class in the trade. This was happening in 1825-26 when there was a speculation mania in the land, and as Beckwith notes, 'rash investments had been made in South American mines, in railways and in gas. In terms of such investments, Scott, Ballantyne, Constable and Hurst and Robinson, were all inextricably connected.

Everything collapsed around Scott, and so came his resolve to fight with his pen. But at the other end of the chain of disaster was James Ogle Robinson, the Leeds Loiner who had seemed to have been a survivor in the cut and thrust world of publishing. However, his firm was declared bankrupt in 1826, and although he found other things, when he died in November, 1837, it must have been with a sense of failure. He had 'made it' in the big city, at least for a few years. One comment about him was that 'He was one of those men whom the world calls enterprising when they succeed, but culpably rash when they fail, and both with a certain reason.'

CHAPTER FIVE

Traditions, Customs and Tall Tales

E VERY ENGLISH SHIRE has its customs and strange examples of popular culture, and Yorkshire is no exception. After all, this is a county which through history has always been intensely agricultural, often idyllically rural, and in places more than a little picturesque. In such poetic locations, it comes as no surprise to learn that some very odd traditions emerged in the countryside communities, and indeed, in very different forms, in the new towns as the West Riding became the centre of the Industrial Revolution.

In matters of custom, of doing what was always the done thing, Yorkshire had been staunchly conservative. The basic, stereotype Yorkie does not like change. The pot of strong tea has to be in the right spot and the armchair has to be placed and angled 'just reet.' Maybe for this fundamental reason, the old customs have persisted, although it must be said that some – such as the traditional 'Mischief Neet' on the evening before Bonfire Night, seems to have largely been erased. But it must be said that much of the old habits and recreational pursuits persist. Many Yorkies still love greyhounds, pigeons and flat caps. The Yorkshireman still had a deep affection for horses ('hosses') and dogs of course. He is not noted for his loquacity, and probably enjoys the peace and quiet of a day's fishing in some green patch of land well away from roads and factories, but he wouldn't shout it out to all and sundry of course.

Tall Tales to Beat them All!

In March, 1890, in Newtown Road, Hobart, out in what was known in crime history as Van Dieman's land, there died a certain Thomas Jennings. This might seem like the opening of an Ozzy story, but Jennings was a Yorkshireman, and indeed one who figures prominently in the annals of Yorkshire tall tales – mainly because he was a heavyweight of 460 pounds.

He was born in Yorkshire in 1824, and although his father was a heavy man, he was nowhere near his son in the statistics of size and proportion in humans. Thomas grew rapidly, and the story is that he laboured long and hard, thinking that would take off some pounds, but in fact the harder he worked, the more weight he put on. He was never less than 33 stones in his adult life. His waist measured 82 inches and his chest was 68 inches; although only 5' 10" in height, he had a circumference at the calf of over 20 inches. One writer in Victorian times states, ' The superabundant flesh was equally distributed, from his double chin to his huge fingers. His face was clear and his eyes bright, and he was the embodiment of good humour and genial intelligence.'

Although this is the tale of a Yorkie, it has to be said that he became a star in Australia of course. The same writer as quoted above explains his celebrity: 'No figure was better known in Hobart than that of Jennings. Whenever he appeared among the audience at the Theatre Royal or the Town Hall... his entrance was always the signal for a burst of welcome. In the hall, two chairs, placed front to front, usually sufficed for his accommodation; but in the theatre the dress circle seats were much too narrow and frail for the purpose. Accordingly, both folding doors were thrown open to their widest extent to give him admission...'

But the county also has another giant in its historical records: William Bradley of Market Weighton. He died in 1820 aged only thirty-three. William was 7'8" tall and weighed 33 stones when he was just nineteen. He had twelve siblings but none of these was exceptionally tall or heavy. Unfortunately, because he was very tall as well as very heavy, William was ideal to star as a celebrity in the then popular 'Freak shows' that the Regency audiences loved so much. His home still survives and was in fact last up for sale in 2006. Little would he have ever suspected that his life would become a 'heritage' feature.

Potter Thompson

Of all the great series of English myths, tales of King Arthur stand out as being constantly fascinating and appealing. The tales are told in all corners of the kingdom, but Yorkshire has its own, and this concerns a certain Potter Thompson at Richmond.

The story of Arthur and his knights waking from their long sleep to come and save England lives on, and that famous line 'the once and future king' sums up the old belief. Perhaps the most well-known location for this is at Cadbury hill fort in Somerset where Arthur allegedly slept inside, and he hunted on a track nearby. There are other traditions too, such as the one fixed at Alderley Edge in Cheshire, which concerns a man taking a white horse to sell when he was stopped by a stranger who pressed him to sell the beast to him. As he would not sell, he was told that he would have no success. Returning, still with the horse, he was led into the hillside to a place where men were asleep, and all but one had a white horse. The man left the horse for Arthur and his men.

This is all about the sleeping lords, and sure enough, a similar tale exists at Richmond. Here, Potter Thompson was accosted by a stranger and led to an underground area where the king and the lords were asleep. Potter was given a sword, along with a horn, and the sword was in its sheath. The stranger told Potter that if he blew the horn and drew the sword, then the assembled group would wake up. The problem was that Potter started to pull the sword, but then his courage failed him when the king and his men began to move and come awake. He put the sword back in, and the sleepers returned to the land of nod. From nowhere, a strange voice called out to the man that he was a despicable coward. Potter ran for it.

The story goes that Potter, much later, tried to go back to the hill and to find the sleepers, but there was no way that he could find the enchanted spot. Arthur has supposedly slept in many places, including places in Scotland and Wales, but in Yorkshire it is cause for some embarrassment that our Yorkie representative, Potter, lost his resolve at the vital moment.

Crying Down the Militia

Back in Victorian times, when the local and regional militias were a prominent part of life, and citizens across the land would have been aware of their presence on manoeuvres, these soldiers on the doorstep were important and highly valued. Nowhere is this perhaps more true than in the beautiful market town of Beverley. In

The Beverley Militia arrive in town
The Graphic

that town, the residents were used to all kinds of Yorkshire traditions, but few were as public and rowdy as the 'crying down' of the militia.

A writer reported on this event in June, 1890, for The *Daily Graphic*, and 'A Beverlonian' gave a vivid account of what happened at this 'warning ceremony' as it was also called, which happened when the men were on the field 'under canvas' at nearby Hurn:

...the big drum, the side-drum, the fife and the tall sergeant, 'Big Ben' – go thundering down the street, making as much clatter as their united and most strenuous exertions will achieve. At every few hundred yards the order 'Halt!' is given. A burst of special violence is indulged in by the drums and fife, and then in the silence which succeeds, the sergeant proceeds to give solemn notice that Colonel Grimston will not be answerable for any debts contracted by the men during the encampment.

Of course, all this pomp is reinforcing the view that the militiamen are not exactly flowing with ready cash, and Beverley was a town rich in hostelries and taverns. In fact, as the same writer puts it, 'the financial worthlessness of the men... was ruthlessly laid bare' and after that admission, the business ended with a rendition of 'God Save the Queen.'

All the tradesmen and landlords of Beverley were then fully informed that there was no hope of much ready money coming their way, and the command to march was given and off went the procession again, as loud as ever. The 'Beverlonian' concludes with the comment that 'Familiar as the good people of Beverley are with the ceremony, this 'crying down' never fails to excite lively interest, and people flock to their doors and windows to hear the fulmination against the 'lads in red.'

The tradition no doubt relates to the long-standing historical associations of the militia musters and the depredations made on the local traders, as the men gathered for some serious bonding and no doubt the pack mentality took over, as the fighting men were released from their usual drudgery for the camp and the playing at soldiers that the exercises entailed. In the last decades of the Victorian years, the country was not short of such military assemblies: as well as militia there were countless riflemen's clubs, amateur fighters and of course, boys' bands and sporting gentlemen, all keen to enjoy playing war. It was in that period that the

Prussian army introduced the 'War Game' to the British, and lectures and demonstrations were given at military bases. The 'crying down' was an announcement to the local people that games were afoot and that thirsty men were about to descend on the streets.

Riding t'Stang and t'Ducking Stool

British folklore is riddled with stories of what is often called 'social moral condemnation.' That is, in various parts of the land, the neighbours expressed their disapproval of such shenanigans as adultery or unfair dealing by noisy and often violent means. In days of yore, the law of the land was not the only source of retribution if there was a transgressor in town.

Riding the Stang

One Yorkshire custom in this respect was called 'riding t'stang' and John Mayhall, writing in 1861, explains: 'This custom was very common during the last century, and may even now be occasionally witnessed in the neighbouring villages of Leeds. A wanton wag, with plenty of gab, is carried through the streets on a stang or pole, followed by all the rag-tag of the village with old tin cans and sticks, drumming and shouting as they march along. When the 'nomine' is to be repeated they halt, while the wag aforesaid pronounces aloud some doggerel lines, beginning,

> *Ran tan tan-*
> *It's neither your cause nor ours that we should ride the stang;*
> *For you may hear by the sound of my frying-pan*
> *That Mistress... has beat her good man...*

In folklore, this carry-on is generally known as 'ran-tanning' and has its local variations across the land. Usually, after the above-mentioned parade, the children round off the occasion by shouting and then running further on to another street where the business is all repeated. The climax was that, as an effigy of the offending person had been made, that item was burned, and the crowd shouted 'sarves her reight!'

Then of course, there is the punishment of the ducking stool. John Mayhall has some examples to give in order to explain this horrendous local punishment given to nagging wives:

> At the court of quarter sessions at Leeds about this time [1690] it was ordered that Anne, the wife of Philip Saule, a person of lewd behaviour, be ducked for daily making strife and discord amongst her neighbours. The like order was made against Jane Miller and Elizabeth Wooller. The punishment of the Ducking Stool is very ancient. In the time of Henry III it was termed 'Tomberell' or 'Tumbrel' and it was afterwards called the 'trebucket' or 'cucking stool.' There was a duckingstool at Quarry Hill, Leeds... At Morley there was one situated somewhere near where the pinfold is, and was removed to Morley Hole...

Naturally, this kind of punishment declined along with similar law-sanctioned retribution such as the stocks and the pillory, but previously these were used as part of the general legal system, the aim being to shame and apply a stigma to misdemeanours.

In his recollections of the village of Ingleton, written in 1893, Anthony Hewitson recalled similar customs: 'Delinquents are at odd times "gibbeted" by fun-loving, scene relishing residents. Ten or a dozen years ago a stout little man who had, it was reported, been showing too much regard for the spouse of a local collier, was tarred and feathered, then fastened to a long strong pole, and in that way carried through the village. And as late as November 1891 the effigies of a married man and a single woman were taken through the village on a cart, the effigies being supported by a lad. He stood between them and rang a bell to attract public attention. Afterwards the effigies were conveyed to a neighbouring eminence where they were blown up with gunpowder and then set on fire.'

What a Snozzle!

Noses and their peculiarities have provided more than freakish faces. After all, Edmond Rostand's great play, *Cyrano de Bergerac* (1897) depends for much of its interest on the long nose of its eponymous hero. Long noses are today forever linked with telling fibs of course. But the Victorians took a wider interest in the organ of smell.

In 1896, a detailed analysis appeared in *The Strand* magazine, explaining the specific clues to personality that could be found in nose types. This was written by a man with the striking name of Stackpool O'Dell, and he was clearly an authoring on the nose, giving examples of such traits as those of Beethoven's nose: 'This nose, like Luther's, seems to denote strength... The head indicates much of the spiritual and the imaginative. The temperament, of which the nose is largely indicative, is the vital, denoting strong recuperative powers, which are very necessary to the supplying of the nervous force expended in musical composition.'

On the other hand, Dickens's nose showed 'sympathy, love and hope.' Stackpool does not venture in to the area of describing the noses of rogues and villains. But where there are oddities, he does not hesitate to find a Yorkshire example. This is in the shape of a man called Thomas Wedders, or Wadhouse (Stackpool is not sure). Wedders had a nose with a length of 7½ inches, and according to Stackpool, 'he exhibited it throughout Yorkshire.' Of course, the writer had to include some critical remarks, as the North tended to be subject to that kind of thing: 'Thus, if noses were ever uniformly exact in representing the importance of the individual, this worthy ought to have amassed all the money in Threadneedle Street and conquered all Europe, for this prodigious nose of his was a compound of the acquisitive with the martial. But either his chin was too weak or his brow too low, or Nature had so exhausted herself in the task of giving this prodigy a nose as to altogether forget to endow him with brains; or, perhaps, the nose crowded out this latter commodity.'

Stackpool could not avoid the extreme negative comment, linking Mr Wedders to the peer group of Shakespearean fools and country yokels of popular humour, as he concludes with, '... we are told the Yorkshireman expired, nose and all, as he had lived, in a condition of mind best described as idiocy the most abject.'

Age Cannot Wither Them

Yorkshire has always been one of those counties that seems to attract or achieve stories of longevity, and one or two Yorkies have gone down in the records of established 'long innings' lives in the history books. In the late Victorian years, one journal made a special investigation into these records, and their findings are staggering. Pride of place was given to Mary Wright, grandmother of the alderman George Tatham. Though born in Edinburgh, she moved to Yorkshire and it was in Leeds that she died, aged 104, on 14 March, 1859.

Mary had known some tough times. One part of the report on her states, 'Mary Wright, when young, removed to London, involving a journey of about two weeks over roads like bullock-tracks in the Transvaal, sleeping for a few hours each night at some inn on the road, and at the end arriving worn out with fatigue..' Her story attracted a few apocryphal elements too, such as the tale that once in a street she was tapped on the arm and turned to see a Quaker lady who said to her, 'Be thou faithful unto death, and I will give thee a crown of life.'

Her life became eventful to say the least. The account in the journal notes that she spent time across the Atlantic: '... after some years she removed with her husband and youngest son to America where she spent sixteen years, mostly in Pennsylvania and Ohio, encountering the hardships of a settler's life... In attending her yearly meetings (as a Quaker) she several times crossed the Alleghany mountains on horseback, having at times to swim the rivers, she being kept on the saddle by a man-Friend on either side.'

Mary Wright, longevity star
Old Yorkshire journal 1880

In the same journal, a certain E.D. Booth of Huddersfield, reported that there had been thirteen persons since 1670 in the village of Kirkburton who had reached the age of at least 95, and that the widow Lee of Broome Bank Steele, clocked up 112 years. Other healthy parts of the county as logged at that time were Pudsey, Whitby and Skipton.

C.T. Oxley, a determined collector of Tyke tales, contributed a notable character to this list of long-in-the-tooth folk. This was Peg Pennyworth, who came into a fortune back in the mid-eighteenth century. She lived in York but loved to be in Scarborough whenever she could manage it, and the latter place was the location of one of her unusual deeds. She set about having a massive meat pie made. Oxley explains, ' Peg instructed her footman to carry it to the bake house. The fellow, however, had other ideas and refused to walk through the streets with the pie, deeming such a mission to be far below his dignity. The coachman also refused to carry the pie to the bake house, considering such an undertaking as unsuitable for one of his station. 'Then bring me the carriage' ordered Peg, and seating herself with true dignity, and holding the pie on her lap, Margaret Wharton [her real name] was driven to the bake house to the amusement of the onlookers.'

Peg lived to be 103, dying in 1791.

Jenkins, the record-holder for sheer old age
Old Yorkshire 1879

But if we really need to recall a staggering achievement in longevity, we have to turn attention to Henry Jenkins. Here was a true record-holder. He was born in Ellerton-upon-Swale near Catterick in 1500, and he died on 9 December, 1670. So he lived for 169 years. In 1880, a writer stated: 'The proofs on which the great age of Jenkins have been examined and sifted with the greatest severity and care, in order, if possible, to detect the slightest fallacy; but the fact appears to be established beyond the reach of reasonable doubt.'

Jenkins was a farm labourer most of his life, and when he was older he took to thatching and fishing. Various people over the years wrote about him, notably a certain Anne Savile, who wrote, 'When I first came to live at Bolton it was told me that there lived in that parish a man near one hundred and fifty years old; that he had sworn as a witness in a cause at York, to one hundred and twenty years, which the judge reproving him for, he said he was butler at that time to Lord Conyers... and it was reported that his name was found in some old register of Lord Conyers' menial servants.'

As later writers noted with astonishment, Jenkins was twelve years old when the Battle of Flodden took place in 1513, and he was still very much mentally alert and working when Charles I was executed. A writer called Grainge, from Harrogate, noted that 'His lifetime appears like that of a nation, more than an individual, so long extended and crowded with such great events.'

Trouble at t' Asylum

To Wakefield people, the words 'Stanley Royd' have that dark resonance that always used to come with a passing reference to the local mental asylum. Possibly anyone from anywhere could name a similar place and recall, in the old, unreformed days when spades were called spades, and equivalent mental institutions. In fact the very word 'institution' used to carry connotations of despair, misery and a hard regime not unlike that of the worst kind of prison. In the case of Stanley Royd, its story was told in a little book written by A.L. Ashworth some years ago, and in that publication we have the tale of the trouble associated with the 'Corpse Road.'

The Corpse Road was an ancient route used, as the name implies, as the route from Stanley to the Wakefield parish church burial ground. As it had such an old established nature and respect, any talk of covering it or denying access to it would cause problems, and this was to be the case after 1819 when the local magistrates decided that the time had come to close the road as its use was interfering with the asylum and becoming a nuisance in their eyes. Seven years later the road was indeed closed and a gate locked. That was asking for a confrontation and they got one. The first incident was that the locals smashed the gate so that a corpse could be carried through. Then matters escalated.

A.L. Ashworth describes what happened: 'The asylum authorities replied by cutting a trench nine feet wide... and nine feet deep. When next they wished to use the road the inhabitants of Stanley promptly filled in the trench, smashed down the gates and passed through, repeating the procedures on the return journey.'

By 1831 matters had deteriorated to such an extent that the local Constable was called in to face a huge mob of three thousand people who were enraged at the repeatedly forced closure of their right of way. Sadly, they were, of course, breaking the law in the way they opposed the locking of the gate and the digging of the trenches. When, in September 1831 the most prominent agitators were arrested and charged, there was a riot. A select bunch of troublemakers were taken for trial at the Leeds Assizes, and it seems that the authorities took a lenient view. Ashworth comments that the thought of a stretch in a house of correction frightened the malefactors; yet whatever the facts, the accused were contrite and released.

In 1849 the cause of the trouble was removed permanently, because a new asylum was built and the old road covered over.

CHAPTER SIX

Show Time!

YORKSHIRE FOLK LOVE a good 'turn' and a show. The county has a long and colourful history of lapping up travelling shows such as burlesques, pantos, slapstick comedy, pageants, parades and feasts. The working men's clubs always had their 'turns' on a Friday night, when locals would do their party-pieces and the result was a local version of 'Britain's Got Talent.' But there were also the real, professional theatres, and they have their story too. It comes as no surprise to a Yorkshire person that both the Batley Variety Club and the Leeds City Varieties became world-famous, and had many of the great names of popular entertainment treading their boards over the years.

The Georgian Theatre Royal and the Palace of Varieties

This wonderful little theatre in North Yorkshire's Richmond is the second oldest working theatre in Britain, following the Bristol Old Vic, which was opened in 1766, but as historians point out, the theatre at Richmond has never been remodelled, whereas at Bristol there have been changes. Other places have their curiosities in the footnotes of the entertainment business, like the converted public toilet in Malvern, which is now a theatre of convenience. But Richmond has its Georgian stage, and it is still a living, working theatre, not a historical curiosity.

Georgian Theatre, Richmond

It was built by Samuel Butler in 1788, in those days when the energetic actor-managers ran the trade, and he had a whole circuit of theatres, from Whitby to Beverley. Up to the late Regency years it was used every week, but in 1848 it was only used as an auction room, and also some wine-vaults were installed. But in the 1960s, the power of a trust was put behind the pressure for its renewal as a theatre and in 1963 it was re-launched. More developments were undertaken, and in 2003 it enjoyed a modernisation process which has brought it into the modern world in terms of facilities, while the original feel of the place for playgoers has been preserved. Great performers have trod the boards there, from Edmund Kean to Alan Bennett and Joyce Grenfell.

The first play to be presented after reopening was fresh from London, and had major stars. This was Sir John Vanbrugh's comedy, *The Provok'd Wife*, and it starred Eileen Atkins, Ann Bell, June Brown, Dinsdale Landen and Trevor Martin, all with the Oxford Playhouse.

The auditorium is of course its main attraction, with a capacity of over 200 seats, boxes on three sides and still, in photos taken for tourists, having the famous 'woodland scene' back-drop which was created in the years between 1818 and 1836. On the reopening, the press reporters were not slow to point out the traditional fun of the night at the theatre in Georgian times, when the pit members could make their presence felt. As one writer explained, 'In the search for accuracy, special electric lights have been brought from France to re-create the candle-lit atmosphere. People in the front row will be able to vent their displeasure in a traditional manner: the theatre's "kicking boards", the double-panelled front of the gallery, still exist to receive foot-stamping disapproval.' Originally, the plan was to produce an obscure piece called *Inkle and Yorico* by George Colman, which had been part of the five-hour opening night back in 1788.

But back in 1962 there was a general air of optimism. Unfortunately, as I write this, there are murmurings in the press that all is not well at the theatre and that it is once again under threat. The ghost of Samuel Butler must be restless.

Leeds City Varieties, the entrance nestling off Briggate and easy to pass by, began as a 'singing room' as part of the White Swan public house, opening for business in June, 1865. Thornton the arcades man owned it, but he sold it in 1876, by auction. It was leased to John Stanfield and then passed to his daughter. In 1894 the place acquired the name City Varieties, and it became known to millions well beyond Leeds when television cameras filmed the series, *The Good Old Days* from there.

It's possible to trace the story back even further, because in 1760 when the White Swan was built, the 'singing room' clearly involved all kinds of 'turns' for customers of all levels and kinds. In 1908 the Ordnance Survey map shows the area it covered, and we know that there was a balcony as part of it, and that it had a capacity to house an audience of 2000 people. There was even a snooker room somewhere within its walls.

In 1880 Stansfield put his name to the concern, letting it be known as Stansfield's Varieties. It became part of a larger outfit when Charles Morritt took over in 1880, as he owned other similar properties. But by that important date of 1894 it was Leeds City Varieties Music Hall to the locals. In 1898 the Empire Theatre was constructed just along the road in Briggate and therefore the Varieties was sold. But the new owner wanted to maintain the music hall tradition and it was re-opened in 1898, run by J. C. Whiteman. Music halls were booming in the 'Naughty Nineties' and some of the personalities who trod the boards in Leeds in that decade were Charlie Chaplin, Lily Langtry the Jersey Belle and even Houdini, about to experience his failure with the Tetley challenge. It was a time when there was a deep interest in regional identity and 'difference' so dialect performers in songs, comic monologues and sketches were popular. An example was the 'Eight Lanacashire Lads' – one of whom was Chaplin. But there was also the Lancashire comedian Morny Cash.

Fred Wood had been in charge, and he had also run the Queen's Theatre in Holbeck, but he died in 1913 and the main opposition to success then was the coming of the silent films. Across the country, a number of music halls were so much in the middle of hard times that they were demolished, but not so the Varieties: it struggled on, though not perhaps with the usual class of stars performing. It really was the age of variety: even to the extent of acts being 'novelty' – a term that covered a variety of sins as well as stars. Certainly that trend is exemplified by the work of Bryant and Bryant, billed as 'Australia's Novelty Manipulators.' They were the Edwardian equivalent of David Copperfield or similar today. Of course, there was always another dimension to variety and that was entirely local. This was a tradition that carried on well into the twentieth century, as in the 'turns' put on every week at Working Men's Clubs' when local talent had its chance. In 1913 the Varieties gave locals an opportunity to entertain by holding amateur wrestling matches: something that accessed the 'gala' or 'company sports day' trend.

Stephen Griffin, in his biography of Ken Dodd, has described the acts in the great age of variety in the Edwardian years:

> *Some of the variety acts were downright bizarre: along with the usual tumblers, acrobats, fire-eaters, jugglers, ventriloquists, dog-acts, contortionists and conjurers there was, for instance, a man who appeared on stage dressed in a voluminous coat, within which was contained virtually any train ticket or card that anyone could name; his whole act was based on audience members calling out the most obscure journey they could imagine…*

The entrepreneur Harry Joseph took over in the middle of the Second World War, leasing it from the White Swan Estate Company. It carried on regardless of the bombs and air-raid warnings. One story told is that a woman gave birth to a child in the audience of one occasion, and Harry Joseph is supposed to have given the child free admission to the theatre for life. From the Joseph era came Frankie Vaughan, real name Frankie Abelson (who was apparently a big hit with the Leeds University Rag review) and lots more who would today be called probably C List celebrities. On the other hand, the playbills tell the story of who was appearing there and some of them are still widely known and fondly remembered from the era of the music halls' golden days – performers such as Arthur Lucan (known to children everywhere at the Saturday Matinees as 'Old Mother Riley'), 'Monsewer Eddie Gray' and even, in 1957, Harry Corbett and Sooty. Many are now forgotten, such as 'Shogun and Rider – Sharpshooters' on the playbill in the 1930s.

Many singers and performers were destined to 'make it' in the world of variety, theatre or operetta, and their stories are often extraordinary, such as that of Lilian Neilson, of whom an early biography said:

> The story of Lilian Neilson's life is largely a story of hardship and sorrow. She was born out of wedlock, in or near Leeds, March 3 (probably) 1846. Her father's name is unknown, her mother, an actress was Miss Brown ... she was reared in humble circumstances and worked in a factory.

But the theatre stories are often charming 'rags to riches' ones and Neilson somehow 'Obtained a footing in the theatre and little by little she made her way to a position of some influence.' Her first big break was playing Juliet at Margate. So many of the Varieties people had lives that would compare to that.

In 1953 the theatre was used for a pilot programme on the old time music hall, and it was a big hit. Joseph, not long before that had been desperate to bring in the punters, and had resorted to having striptease acts. This was still the time when the girls had to form a tableaux picture and not move any limbs. But such moves became outdated when, in 1953, *The Good Old Days* was broadcast and the Varieties never looked back. The show was devised by Barney Coleman, Leeds based, who had also produced the Wilfred Pickles programme, *Have a Go*. In 1890, three pence entry fee entitled a customer to a glass of beer, a seat and a right to hurl abuse at performers who did not come up to scratch. By 1973, when celebrating the twenty years of the programme's success, it also held a long pantomime season of nineteen weeks.

The BBC took two days to record a show, having to remove some of the seats to install cameras in position. The stars rehearsed on a Sunday and the band was called on by the afternoon, and then the whole show recorded on the Sunday night, so the BBC men were packing up by Monday. The *compere* was Mr Leonard Sachs, known as the man who 'dined on dictionaries' and one of the traditional activities of the show was the crowd jeering him as he spewed out strings of alliterative compliments about the performers. In 1973 there was a waiting list of 20,000 people to attend and don the Edwardian costume, only too keen to shout and heckle when required, and certainly to join in the hearty choruses.

The Varieties had hosted hundreds of forgotten performers, but it has to be said that very famous people have entertained there. One of the classic acts was that of the great Sir Harry Lauder, who appeared in Leeds in 1911 and was paid the sum of £11 and said to be 'rather good'. Since then almost every well-known singer from cabaret and club land has appeared there, along with the comics of the Ken Dodd variety. The Varieties is without doubt a major Leeds institution, quite easy to pass and overlook, but the cultural historians will never let it be forgotten. It has recently been refurbished, after being sold to Leeds City Council in 1987, and it looks as though, if advertising is to be believed, that *The Good Old Days* is making a comeback.

Mr John Dunn and the Titanic Band's Violins

Everything related to the ill-fated *Titanic* now has great value and of course, much general interest. Only last year (2015) I saw a table napkin

John Dunn, the violinist

from that giant liner for sale, framed and under glass, for £300. But so many of the everyday objects that went down have a hidden story, and this is about one of them – possessions of a musician who went down with her.

In his theatrical agent's brochure of 1900, John Dunn was given a very impress-ive blurb:

> *Mr Dunn is a native of Yorkshire, but at the age of twelve he went to Leipzig to study under the celebrated violinist and teacher, Schradiek... On his return to England three years later he made his appearance at the Covent Garden Promenade Concerts, where he created a tremendous sensation... He has since given concerts throughout the United Kingdom, and has besides a widespread reputation on the Continent.*

Dunn, from Hull, became one of the leading experts on the violin in Britain, and he was praised by the music critics in the broadsheets for years. The *Telegraph* summed up, 'Our English artiste, who supremely asserted a mastery of his instrument, such as few have gained, and fewer can now boast... was the centre of the occasion...' He was the performer who first played Tchaikovsky's violin concerto in Britain, and people went too him for advice and tuition. In fact, this general opinion of his wisdom on matters concerned with the violin led to his being involved in a story from the ill-fated liner, the *Titanic*.

Although Dunn was well known in his time in classical music circles, he seldom figured on the larger stage of history. But there is one exception. As is known, almost as a mythic story, when the *Titanic* went down beneath the ice-cold sea in April, 1912, the band played on until their last moments. But there were survivors and there were angry relatives, and when the furore was over, there were practical matters such as insurance to settle. Some valuable musical instruments were lost of course, and among these were violins.

Before his fateful work on the liner, Andrew Hume, a violinist with the ship's band and contracted by Black's, a musical agent in Liverpool, had been something of a campaigner for the valuation and comparability of the famous, older violins of the Italian craftsmen, and their modern counterparts, and he had written several times on the subject to a journal called *The Strad* on this. After his death, his father found himself in the sad situation of so many after that disaster: he had no compensation claim. His son, being contracted to Black's was not an employee of the White Star Line and could not claim. There was a hearing at the county court against the Black agency and the claimants lost.

Mr Hume wrote to the White Star Line, and even to Bruce Ismay, the chairman and managing director of the line who had been on the ship and who had survived, asking for recompense; after all, his son and the other musicians had bravely gone down, playing *Nearer my God to Thee* as the waves engulfed them. Mr Hume needed to have some kind of argument that the violins his son owned were valuable, and so the past was explored. There was an opinion expressed by John Dunn about modern violins and some older ones and he had used the phrase, 'both your violins are exceedingly fine' and of course, this was useful back-up in any application for money.

But alas, none of this pleading or demanding worked. Dunn's opinion would be valued, of course, but nothing could persuade the White Star Line that a young musician had taken very expensive instruments with him on that last voyage.

The Almanac Man

In Victorian times, after the massive move to the towns during the Industrial Revolution, the vast new ranks of the new urban workers became a new audience for all kinds of entertainments, on the stage and on the page, in the circus-field or at the travelling feast. It was a time, that early Victorian period through to the Edwardian years, when the whole world seemed to want to be entertained. There was every

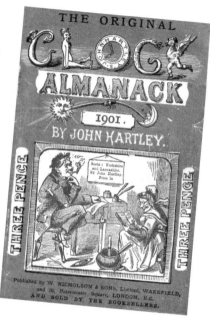

Cover of Hartley's Clock Almanack

variety of show on offer, from the music halls to serious theatre and from freak shows to penny gaffs, and in the midst of all this, in Yorkshire and Lancashire, there were the working class literary entertainments on offer.

This material, in the northern dialects on most occasions, helped to create some celebrities: these were poets and speakers who could fill the hall of a mechanics' institute or a chapel for a 'Penny Reading' and their dialect poems would raise a laugh, delivered in the same words which the mill workers and colliers heard every day at work and at home. One of the great stars of this scene was John Hartley, the man who started the famous Yorkshire publication, *The Clock Almanack*. That is how it was spelled, with a final 'k.' That made it somehow ordinary but extraordinary at the same time. The cover illustration suggested earthy humour and everyday tales. Into the almanac went the same tales that Hartley delivered in his readings, and it all worked very well.

Who was this character? Thanks to his biographer, Rod Dimbleby, we know much more about him now. He was born in Halifax in 1839 and died in Cheshire in 1915. He left school at twelve and began as a pattern designer at a textile firm. He married young and that did not work out; he left for America and married again and worked as a carpet designer, but a major economic crash ruined him. Back in England, he concentrated on the new career which was to make his name.

There were many characteristics of the almanacs, with their rich humour and entertaining tales, but above all, one might say, there was the pull of the maxim or scrap of homely wisdom, and Hartley specialised in that; in his words we have the absolute epitome of the kind of Yorkshire wisdom we have in tourist and heritage sites today, from Bronteland to the shops in York. For instance, we have the simplicity of 'Don't live as if this world were all, for t' time will come one day / when that grim messenger will call' or 'It's grand to have plenty of brass / then t'parsons know where you live / If you're poor it's most likely they'll pass.'

As Rod notes, at the heart of the almanac's philosophy is the 'plain blunt Yorkshireman.' We might sum this up, as Hartley did, with, 'My life has been a long sermon on "Mak thy best of it."'

Hartley did more than most to promote Yorkshire to the world, notably between c.1880 and 1900 when the *Clock* was really popular. He was the kind of man who would find humour in anything: perhaps, one might say, Yorkshire's own version of Mark Twain. In terms of his Yorkshire readership, he was a mega-star, but now he is forgotten by all but a few enthusiasts. Still, his work represents something quintessentially Tyke – the love of telling a good tale.

Strange Shows Indeed: Wife Sales

In the years before Hardwick's Marriage Act of 1753, it was considered by many poor people that, as a divorce could only be obtained by an Act of Parliament, a public statement of a separation would release individuals from marital turmoil and unhappiness. But the law relating to such deeds was always equivocal, and custom changed in different localities. Whatever the general opinion of such things, the sale of a wife became a fairly common practice. It has to be remembered that until the late nineteenth century, a wife was the property of her husband.

Every corner of Britain has its stories of the sale of wives. Back in the day, such things were not rare, and in fact Thomas Hardy, in his novel, *The Mayor of Casterbridge*, makes such an event a memorable part of his story. The historian combing the local papers in Georgian and Victorian times will most likely find accounts of such sales. These strange retail outlets took place sometimes as a 'show' – a public auction in fact.

Such was the case in 1806 when George Gowthorp from Patrington, had his wife put up for sale in Hull. This took place in the market square and a man paid 20 guineas for her. In a note that sends a fire of indignation through the modern reader, it is on record that the buyer led away his woman with a halter round her neck, like a prize heifer. Nine years later, at Pontefract, a wife was sold for seven shillings, and there were other such affairs around that time. But in 1837, at the West Riding Quarter Sessions, Joshua Jackson was convicted of this: it had become a criminal offence and he served a month in jail.

Still, illegal or not, wife sales went on, and as late as 1888, there was a press report of a wife sale at Little Horton, near Bradford. The husband was called Hartley Thompson, and he had asked the public bellman to announce the event. The *Stamford Mercury* reported what happened: 'The wife, it is said, appeared before the crowd with a halter adorned with ribbons round her neck. The sale, however, was not completed, the reason for this being that some disturbance was created by a crowd from a nearby factory and that the person to whom it was intended to sell the wife (Ike

Duncan) was detained by his wife before the time. The couple, though not long wedded, have had a very unhappy life and it is said that they were so egregiously ignorant as to believe that they could secure their own legal separation by such an absurd course – a public sale.'

Unbelievably, there was one attempted sale, in 1858, when someone put in a first bid of one and a half penny. In contrast, *The Gentleman's Magazine* in 1832 reported that the Duke of Chandos, after seeing a wife being beaten by her ostler husband, and then offered for sale, bought the woman, gave her an education, and then later married her.

Those Magnificent Men... and Women

At the height of the Edwardian good times, when playboys indulged in all their favourite sports such as hunting, shooting and fishing, lots of new enterprises came along to entertain the wealthy and the idle rich. One man in the ranks of the adventurers of the time, however, who was rarely idle and never really rich, was Harry de Windt, the author of the compellingly-titled travel work, *From Paris to New York by Land*. One highlight in his sporting life was the latest technical obsession of gentlemen of adventure – flying. In 1909 Doncaster took centre stage in this area of sport and technology, as the town hosted the first aviation meeting in Great Britain, using the expanse of the famous racecourse, home of the classic St Leger.

Most of the celebrity flying aces and adventurers of the day were invited, including the French contingent, led by Roger Sommer and Leon Delagrange; also appearing was the flamboyant Samuel F. Cody, showman and brother of the famous Buffalo Bill Cody. He had taken up flying during the period when his Wild West Show was in Britain, and he clearly had a flair for the business. He met with the other international aviators for most of the month of October, and Harry was one of the stewards at the meeting.

In Harry's recollection, the affair was a 'fiasco' and he notes that the weather was dismal, but that seems to be a grumpy point of view. Later writers on the air show describe it as being quite sensational. Every flyer was paid the huge sum of £200 for taking part, and the real entertainers in the ranks of the competitors surely made those weeks memorable. Harry recalled Cody vividly: 'One day, however, the late Captain Cody [he was killed while flying in 1913] valiantly braved a scarcely perceptible breeze, and rose amidst deafening cheers, in a cumbersome plane which rattled like a threshing machine, to proceed a short distance about sixty feet high, and then fall heavily to the ground...'

He also recalls some trouble at that event, explaining that a Yorkshire crowd in the shilling stands rioted and tore down the railings; he claimed that 'they swarmed onto the course, intent upon mobbing everyone concerned with the venture, until dispersed by a strong force of police.' Harry was negatively selective on this experience: he does not mention the fact that Delagrange, flying his Bleriot monoplane, won the Inauguration Cup and he exceeded the world air-speed record, reaching over 53 m.p.h. in front of the Doncaster crowd.

The Doncaster event was very successful, and the next year, women aviators were very much in the limelight: Helene Dutrieu starred then, as she had proved her mettle by flying from Ostend to Bruges. In Doncaster, three male and three female pilots engaged in some good-humoured competition, and Helene was in that entertainment. The pictures taken at the time show that the women pilots attracted plenty of attention; after all, this was a time when the Suffragettes were busy breaking the law while at the same time (in 1919) legislation was passed which was to open up all kinds of new professions for women. Just ten years after the Doncaster female aces took to the skies, the first woman police officer was sworn in and in 1921 women sat for the first time on the jury in a murder trial.

The Doncaster air display was a sign of great changes to come, and in 1930 Amy Johnson was the first woman to fly solo from England to

Australia. Amy was born in Hull in 1903, went to school at the Boulevard Municipal Secondary School and later gained her B.A. at Sheffield. She set a number of long-distance records, sometimes alone and sometimes with her husband. In the Second World War she flew transport planes, and at her death in 1941 she was a legend. Today she is in the pantheon of Yorkshire heroes and is, of course, the pride of the city of Kingston-upon-Hull.

Acknowledgements and Thanks

Thanks go to all correspondents who have helped in the gathering of some of these tales. In particular, I'd like to acknowledge the contributions of Sue Brown, Amy Lofthouse, Jade McGlynn, Philip Bolton, Julia Spearing, Rod Dimbleby and Joan Shaw. Also staff at the Brymor Jones library, who helped in the search for ephemera.

Bibliography

Yorkshire literature is full of collections of writings dealing with eccentrics, strange happenings and odd events; the Victorians were especially fond of gathering tales of eccentrics, with the same zest as they employed in collecting objects of interest and antiquities. My sources mostly come from such writings, but thanks go to more recent writers too, including C. T. Oxley and various contributors to the letters pages of *The Dalesman* and *Down Your Way* magazines.

Dates of first publication are given in brackets before the date of the referenced text.

Ashworth, A. L., *Stanley Royd Hospital, Wakefield* (The author, no date)

Baring-Gould, S., *Yorkshire Oddities* (1874) (Smith Settle, 1987)

Beckwith, Frank, 'The Leeds Library and Sir Walter Scott' in *The University of Leeds Review* Vol. XI no. 2 Dec, 1968 pp. 152-161

Bentley, John (Ed.), *The Story of my Village, by Anthony Hewitson* (J.Bentley, 1982)

Clay, Jeremy, *The Burglar Caught by a Skeleton* (Icon Books, 2014)

Dimbleby, Rod, *Discovering John Hartley's Clock Almanacks 1867-1916* (Charlesworth Press, 2014)

Graham, Frank, *Old Inns and Taverns of Yorkshire* (V. Graham, 1965)

Gregory, Jeremy and Stevenson, John, *Britain in the Eighteenth Century* (Routledge, 2007)

Harrison, F., *The Story of York Minster* (Herald Printing Works, 1963)

Hartley, John, *The Original Clock Almanack* (W. Nicholson, 1901)

Mayhall, John, *The Annals of Yorkshire* (Joseph Johnson, 1861)

Newbery, Maggie, *Reminiscences of a Bradford Mill Girl* (Bradford Metropolitan Borough Council, 1980)

Oxley, C.T., *A Broadacre Miscellany* (the author, no date)

Oxley, C.T., *Believe it or Not* (The author, no date)

Peacock, A.J., *Essays in York History* (York Educational Settlement, no date)

Sala, George Augustus, *The Life and Adventures of George Augustus Sala* (Cassell, 1895)

Scruton, William, *Pen and Pencil Sketches of Old Bradford* (1890) (Amethyst Press, 1985)

Smith, William (Ed.), *Old Yorkshire* (Longmans Green, 1881)